The Conquest of Poverty

THE

Conquest

of

Poverty

HENRY HAZLITT

ARLINGTON HOUSE   New Rochelle, N.Y.

Fourth Printing, December, 1976

Library of Congress Catalog Card Number 72–9123

ISBN 0–87000–142–6

MANUFACTURED IN THE UNITED STATES OF AMERICA

This volume is a publication of
The Principles of Freedom Committee

Acknowledgments

I wish to express my gratitude to the Principles of Freedom Committee, and also to the Institute for Humane Studies of Menlo Park, California, for their help and encouragement to me in writing this book.

The Committee has promoted a series of books on economic issues that seek to clarify the workings of the free market and the consequences of governmental intervention. I am proud to find my book in the company of the five previous volumes in the Principles of Freedom Series: *Great Myths of Economics* (1968), by Don Paarlberg, *The Strange World of Ivan Ivanov* (1969), by G. Warren Nutter, *Freedom in Jeopardy: The Tyranny of Idealism* (1969), by John V. Van Sickle, *The Genius of the West* (1971), by Louis Rougier, and *The Regulated Consumer* (1971), by Mary Bennett Peterson.

The substance of Chapter 13, "How Unions Reduce Real Wages," was delivered as a talk before the international Mont Pelerin Society at Munich, West Germany, in 1970.

HENRY HAZLITT

Wilton, Connecticut
August, 1972

Contents

The Conquest of Poverty

CHAPTER 1

The Problem of Poverty

THE HISTORY OF POVERTY IS ALMOST THE HISTORY OF MANKIND. THE ancient writers have left us few specific accounts of it. They took it for granted. Poverty was the normal lot.

The ancient world of Greece and Rome, as modern historians reconstruct it, was a world where houses had no chimneys, and rooms, heated in cold weather by a fire on a hearth or a fire-pan in the center of the room, were filled with smoke whenever a fire was started, and consequently walls, ceiling, and furniture were blackened and more or less covered by soot at all times; where light was supplied by smoky oil lamps which, like the houses in which they were used, had no chimneys; and where eye trouble as a result of all this smoke was general. Greek dwellings had no heat in winter, no adequate sanitary arrangements, and no washing facilities.[1]

Above all there was hunger and famine, so chronic that only

1. E. Parmalee Prentice, *Hunger and History*, Harper & Bros., 1939, pp. 39–40.

the worst examples were recorded. We learn from the Bible how Joseph advised the pharaohs on famine relief measures in ancient Egypt. In a famine in Rome in 436 B.C., thousands of starving people threw themselves into the Tiber.

Conditions in the Middle Ages were no better:

"The dwellings of medieval laborers were hovels—the walls made of a few boards cemented with mud and leaves. Rushes and reeds or heather made the thatch for the roof. Inside the houses there was a single room, or in some cases two rooms, not plastered and without floor, ceiling, chimney, fireplace or bed, and here the owner, his family and his animals lived and died. There was no sewage for the houses, no drainage, except surface drainage for the streets, no water supply beyond that provided by the town pump, and no knowledge of the simplest forms of sanitation. 'Rye and oats furnished the bread and drink of the great body of the people of Europe. . . . Precariousness of livelihood, alternations between feasting and starvation, droughts, scarcities, famines, crime, violence, murrains, scurvy, leprosy, typhoid diseases, wars, pestilences and plagues'—made part of medieval life to a degree with which we are wholly unacquainted in the Western world of the present day."[2]

And, ever-recurring, there was famine:

"In the eleventh and twelfth centuries famine [in England] is recorded every fourteen years, on an average, and the people suffered twenty years of famine in two hundred years. In the thirteenth century the list exhibits the same proportion of famine; the addition of high prices made the proportion greater. Upon the whole, scarcities decreased during the three following centuries; but the average from 1201 to 1600 is the same, namely, seven famines and ten years of famine in a century."[3]

2. *Ibid.*, pp. 15–16.
3. William Farr, "The Influence of Scarcities and of the High Prices of Wheat on the Mortality of the People of England," *Journal of the Royal Statistical Society,* February 16, 1846, Vol. IX, p. 158.

One writer has compiled a detailed summary of twenty-two famines in the thirteenth century in the British Isles, with such typical entries as: "1235: Famine and plague in England; 20,000 persons die in London; people eat horse-flesh, bark of trees, grass, etc."[4]

But recurrent starvation runs through the whole of human history. The *Encyclopedia Britannica* lists thirty-one major famines from ancient times down to 1960.[5] Let us look first at those from the Middle Ages to the end of the eighteenth century:

1005: famine in England. *1016:* famine throughout Europe. *1064–72:* seven years' famine in Egypt. *1148–59:* eleven years' famine in India. *1344–45:* great famine in India. *1396–1407:* the Durga Devi famine in India, lasting twelve years. *1586:* famine in England giving rise to the Poor Law system. *1661:* famine in India; no rain fell for two years. *1769–70:* great famine in Bengal; a third of the population—10 million persons—perished. *1783:* the Chalisa famine in India. *1790–92:* the Deju Bara, or skull famine, in India, so called because the dead were too numerous to be buried.

This list is incomplete—as probably any list would be. In the winter of 1709, for example, in France, more than a million persons, according to the figures of the time, died out of a population of 20 millions.[6] In the eighteenth century, in fact, France suffered eight famines, culminating in the short crops of 1788, which were one of the causes of the Revolution.

I am sorry to be dwelling in such detail on so much human misery. I do so only because mass starvation is the most obvious and intense form of poverty, and this chronicle is needed to remind us of the appalling dimensions and persistence of the evil.

4. Cornelius Walford, "The Famines of the World," *Journal of the Royal Statistical Society,* March 19, 1878, Vol. 41, p. 433.
5. "Famine," *Encyclopedia Britannica,* 1965.
6. Gaston Bouthoul, *La population dans la monde,* pp. 142–43.

In 1798, a young English country parson, Thomas R. Malthus, delving into this sad history, anonymously published an *Essay on the Principles of Population as it affects the Future Improvement of Society.* His central doctrine was that there is a constant tendency for population to outgrow food supply and production. Unless checked by self-restraint, population will always expand to the limit of subsistence, and will be held there by disease, war, and ultimately famine. Malthus was an economic pessimist, viewing poverty as man's inescapable lot. He influenced Ricardo and other classical economists of his time, and the general tone of their writings led Carlyle to denounce political economy as "the Dismal Science."

Malthus had in fact uncovered a truth of epoch-making importance. His work first set Charles Darwin on the chain of reasoning which led to the promulgation of the theory of evolution by natural selection. But Malthus greatly overstated his case, and neglected to make essential qualifications. He failed to see that, once men in any place (it happened to be his own England) succeeded in earning and saving a little surplus, made even a moderate capital accummulation, and lived in an era of political freedom and protection for property, their liberated industry, thought, and invention could at last make it possible for them enormously and acceleratively to multiply per capita production beyond anything achieved or dreamed of in the past. Malthus announced his pessimistic conclusions just in the era when they were about to be falsified.

The Industrial Revolution

The Industrial Revolution had begun, but nobody had yet recognized or named it. One of the consequences of the increased production it led to was to make possible an unparalleled increase in population. The population of England and Wales in 1700 is estimated to have been about 5,500,000; by 1750 it had reached some 6,500,000. When the first census was taken in 1801 it was 9,000,000; by 1831 it had reached 14,000,000. In the second half of the eighteenth century population had thus increased by 40 percent, and in the first three decades of the nineteenth century by more than 50 percent. This was not the result of any marked change in the birth rate, but of an almost continuous fall in the death rate. People were now producing the food supply and other means to support a greater number of them.[7]

This accelerating growth in population continued. The enormous forward spurt of the world's population in the nineteenth century was unprecedented in human experience. "In one century, humanity added much more to its total volume than it had been able to add during the previous million years."[8]

But we are getting ahead of our story. We are here concerned with the long history of human poverty and starvation, rather than with the short history of how mankind began to emerge from it. Let us come back to the chronicle of famines, this time from the beginning of the nineteenth century:

1838: intense famine in North-Western Provinces (Uttar Pradesh), India; 800,000 perished. *1846–47:* famine in Ireland, resulting from the failure of the potato crop. *1861:* famine in northwest India. *1866:* famine in Bengal and Orissa; 1,000,000 perished. *1869:* intense famine in Rajputana; 1,500,000 perished. *1874:* famine in Bihar, India. *1876–78:* famine in Bombay, Madras, and Mysore; 5,000,000 perished. *1877–78:* famine in north China; 9,500,000 said to have perished. *1887–89:* famine in China. *1891–92:* famine in Russia. *1897:* famine in India; 1,000,000 perished. *1905:* famine in Russia. *1916:* famine in China. *1921:* famine in the U.S.S.R., brought on by Communist economic policies; at least 10,000,000 persons seemed doomed to die, until the American Relief Administration, headed by

7. T. S. Ashton, *The Industrial Revolution (1760–1830),* Oxford University Press, 1948, pp. 3–4.
8. Henry Pratt Fairchild, "When Population Levels Off," *Harper's Magazine,* May, 1938, Vol. 176, p. 596.

Herbert Hoover, came in and reduced direct deaths to about 500,000. *1932–33:* famine again in the U.S.S.R., brought on by Stalin's farm collectivization policies; "millions of deaths." *1943:* famine in Bengal; about 1,500,000 perished. *1960–61:* famine in the Congo.[9]

We can bring this dismal history down to date by mentioning the famines in recent years in Communist China and the war-created famine of 1968–70 in Biafra.

The record of famines since the end of the eighteenth century does, however, reveal one striking difference from the record up to that point. Mass starvation did not fall on a single country in the now industrialized Western world. (The sole exception is the potato famine in Ireland; and even that is a doubtful exception because the Industrial Revolution had barely touched mid-nineteenth-century Ireland—still a one-crop agricultural country.)

It is not that there have ceased to be droughts, pests, plant diseases, and crop failures in the modern Western world, but that when they occur there is no famine, because the stricken countries are quickly able to import foodstuffs from abroad, not only because the modern means of transport exist, but because, out of their industrial production, these countries have the means to pay for such foodstuffs.

In the Western world today, in other words, poverty and hunger—until the mid-eighteenth century the normal condition of mankind—have been reduced to a residual problem affecting only a minority; and that minority is being steadily reduced.

But the poverty and hunger still prevailing in the rest of the world—in most of Asia, Central and South America, and Africa—in short, even now afflicting the great majority of mankind—show the terrible dimensions of the problem still to be solved.

And what has happened and is still happening in many countries today serves to warn us how fatally easy it is to destroy all

9. "Famine" and "Russia," *Encyclopedia Britannica,* 1965.

the economic progress that has already been achieved. Foolish governmental interference led the Argentine, once the world's principal producer and exporter of beef, to forbid in 1971 even domestic consumption of beef on alternate weeks. Soviet Russia, one of whose chief economic problems before it was communized was to find an export market for its huge surplus of grains, has been forced to import grains from the capitalist countries. One could go on to cite scores of other examples, with ruinous consequences, all brought on by short-sighted governmental policies.

More than thirty years ago, E. Parmalee Prentice was pointing out that mankind has been rescued from a world of want so quickly that the sons do not know how their fathers lived:

"Here, indeed, is an explanation of the dissatisfaction with conditions of life so often expressed, since men who never knew want such as that in which the world lived during many by-gone centuries, are unable to value at its true worth such abundance as now exists, and are unhappy because it is not greater."[10]

How prophetic of the attitude of rebellious youth in the 1970s! The great present danger is that impatience and ignorance may combine to destroy in a single generation the progress that it took untold generations of mankind to achieve.

"Those who cannot remember the past are condemned to repeat it."

10. *Hunger and History,* p. 236.

CHAPTER 2

Poverty and Population

SINCE THE END OF THE EIGHTEENTH CENTURY EVERY MEANINGFUL study of the causes of poverty has at some point referred to the growth of population. It was the achievement of Malthus to have pointed out the connection in so impressive a way that it could never again be ignored.

The thesis of his first *Essay on Population,* published in 1798, was that dreams of universal affluence were vain, because there was an inevitable tendency for population to exceed the food supply. "Population, when unchecked, increases in a geometrical ratio. Subsistence increases only in an arithmetical ratio." There is a fixed limit to the supply of land and the size of the crop that can be grown per acre. Malthus spells out what he sees as the fateful consequences of this disproportion:

"In the United States of America, where the means of subsistence have been more ample . . . than in any of the modern states of Europe, the population has been found to double itself in twenty-five years. . . . We will take as our rule, and say, that population, when unchecked, goes on doubling itself every twenty-five years, or increases in a geometrical ratio.... Taking the population of the world at any number, a thousand millions, for instance, the human species would increase in the ratio of—1, 2, 4, 8, 16, 32, 64, 128, 156, 512, &c. and subsistence as—1, 2, 3, 4, 5, 6, 7, 8, 9, 10, &c. In two centuries and a quarter the population would be to the means of subsistence as 512 to 10: in three centuries as 4096 to 13. . . .”

This fearful arithmetic led Malthus to a despairing conclusion. He had started with two postulates: “First, that food is necessary to the existence of man. Secondly, that the passion between the sexes is necessary and will remain nearly in its present state.” And as he saw no voluntary way, except a “continence” that he did not believe was possible, to prevent the geometrical increase in population, he concluded that population will always tend to expand to the limit of subsistence and be held there by misery, war, pestilence, and famine. “That population does invariably increase where there are the means of subsistence, the history of every people that ever existed will abundantly prove.”

The appearance of this *Essay* brought down on the author’s head a storm of criticism and vituperation. As a result Malthus published five years later, in 1803, a second edition of the *Essay*. It was much longer—in effect an entirely new book—and it became the basis of the six subsequent editions.

There were two main changes. Malthus attempted to support his original thesis with a great mass of factual data on population growth and checks taken not only from history but from contemporary conditions in a score of other countries. But in addition to bringing in this supporting evidence, Malthus made a concession. “Throughout the whole of the present work,” he wrote in the preface to his second edition, “I have so far differed in principle from the former, as to suppose the action of another check to population which does not come under the head either of vice or misery.” This other check was “moral restraint"—that is, "the restraint from marriage which is not followed by irregular gratifications"—the deliberate restraint of the great majority of mankind, by the use of forethought, prudence and reason, from giving birth as individual couples to an excessive number of children. In contemporary Europe, Malthus now found, moral restraint "was the most powerful of the checks on population."

Hostile critics have contended that in making this concession Malthus in effect abandoned his theory altogether. "The introduction of the prudential check ('moral restraint')", wrote Schumpeter, "makes all the difference. . . . All the theory gains thereby is orderly retreat with the artillery lost."[1] Even a more sympathetic critic like Gertrude Himmelfarb writes:

"Thus the principle of population ceased to be a fatal obstacle to man's dreams and ideals. Indeed the principle itself was no longer as inexorable as he had earlier suggested. It now appeared that population did not necessarily outrun food supply, or necessarily keep up with every increase in food. . . . Men were no longer at the mercy of forces outside their control: 'Each individual has, to a great degree, the power of avoiding the evil consequences to himself and society resulting from it [the principle of population] by the practice of a virtue dictated to him by the light of nature, and sanctioned by revealed religion.' Liberated from the eternal menace of over-population and the eternal evils of misery and vice, society could now look forward to the union of 'the two grand desiderata, a great actual population and a state of society in which abject poverty and dependence are comparatively but little known; two objects which are far from being incompatible.' "[2]

In spite of these quotations from Malthus himself, the contrast between the first and subsequent editions of the *Essay* was

---

1. Joseph A. Schumpeter, *History of Economic Analysis,* Oxford University Press, 1954, p. 580.
2. Introduction to Modern Library edition (1960) of Thomas Robert Malthus, *On Population,* p. xxx.

not as great as these critics imply. The change in tone was greater than the change in substance. Malthus had been stunned by the savagery of the attacks on his despairing conclusions, and wanted to blunt this by emphasizing as much as he could any element of hope. In his first edition he had failed to admit the possibility of a really effective "moral restraint" on the part of the great majority of mankind; in his subsequent editions he did admit that possibility—but certainly not that probability. In fact, as he would have been appalled by the "vice" of our modern mechanical and chemical methods of birth control (now ironically called "neo-Malthusianism"), even if he had foreseen them, how could he have believed in the probability of the almost lifelong refrainment from sexual relations necessary to prevent each couple, without "birth control" methods, from having no more than two or three children?

What Malthus Contributed

The trouble with most discussions of Malthus is that they have tried to prove him either wholly right or wholly wrong. Let us try to see, rather, exactly what he did contribute, and both what was right and what was wrong with it.

The great contribution of Malthus was to be the first to state clearly, and in relation to each other, two very important propositions. The first was the tendency of all populations, animal and human, to increase in the absence of checks at a geometrical ratio—or, in more modern technical terms, at an exponential rate. Malthus spoke of populations doubling every 25 years, in the United States of his day, or every 40 years, say, in the England of his day. He wrote of rates of growth as measured in generations. Today demographers usually discuss population growth in terms of an annual rate. But any percentage rate, if continued, is compounded. A population growing at a rate of "only" 2 percent annually would double itself every 35 years; a population growing at a rate of 3 percent annually would double itself in 24 years; and so on. Some hostile critics of Malthus have attempted to dismiss this proposition as "trivial" or "obvious." Its implications are anything but trivial, and it was obvious only after Malthus pointed it out.

Malthus's second great proposition, based on the limited supply and productivity of land, was in fact the first clear though crude statement in English of what afterward came to be known as "the law of diminishing returns." No statement of this law is to be found in Adam Smith. (A remarkably good formulation of it was made by the French economist Turgot in 1767, but Malthus appears not to have been familiar with it.) By the time we get to John Stuart Mill's *Principles of Political Economy* in 1848, however, we find a careful and qualified statement:

"Land differs from the other elements of production, labor and capital, in not being susceptible of indefinite increase. Its extent is limited, and the extent of the more productive kinds of it more limited still. It is also evident that the quantity of produce capable of being raised on any given piece of land is not indefinite. . . .

"It is commonly thought . . . that for the present limitation of production or population from this source is at an indefinite distance, and that ages must elapse before any practical necessity arises for taking the limiting principle into serious consideration.

"I apprehend this to be not only an error, but the most serious one to be found in the whole field of political economy. The question is more important and fundamental than any other; it involves the whole subject of the causes of poverty. . . .

"After a certain, and not very advanced, stage in the progress of agriculture, it is the law of production from the land, that in *any given state of agricultural skill and knowledge* [italics supplied], by increasing the labor, the produce is not increased in an equal degree; or, to express the same thing in other words, every increase of produce is obtained by a more than proportional increase in the application of labor to the land.

"This general law of agricultural industry is the most important proposition in political economy. . . .

"The produce of land increases, *caeteris paribus,* in a diminishing ratio to the increase in the labor employed."[3]

Several points are to be noticed about this formulation. It discards the unrealistic 1–2–3 "arithmetical" rate of increase of subsistence postulated by Malthus for a more generalized and accurate statement. And it includes the indispensable qualification that I have italicized. The law of diminishing returns applies only to a given state of technical knowledge. Mill constantly emphasized this: "There is another agency in habitual antagonism to the law of diminishing return from land"; this is "no other than the progress of civilization," especially "the progress of agricultural knowledge, skill, and invention."

It is because Malthus overlooked this vital qualification that "Malthusianism" fell into disrepute about half a century after his book appeared and then remained so for a full century. For he was writing practically at the beginning of the Industrial Revolution. During that Revolution (approximately 1760 to 1830) there was an unprecedented increase in the British population and at the same time an unprecedented increase in per capita production. Both of these increases were made possible by the relatively sudden introduction of new productive inventions and techniques. As Malthus's statement had utterly failed to allow for this, the law of diminishing returns was thought to have been proved untenable. Fears of excessive population growth were dismissed as groundless.

It should be pointed out here parenthetically that the law of diminishing returns as applied to land is now seen to be only a special case of a much wider principle governing both increasing and decreasing returns. Decreasing returns do not apply solely to agriculture and mining, as the mid-nineteenth-

3. John Stuart Mill, *Principles,* Book I, Ch. XII.

century economists thought, nor increasing returns specifically to manufacturing. In its modern form the law of returns simply points out that there is an optimum ratio in which, in any given state of technique, two or more complementary factors of production can be employed for maximum output; and that when we deviate from this optimal combination by, say, increasing the quantity of one factor without increasing the quantity of the others, we may indeed get an increase in production, but it will be less than proportionate. The law can be most satisfactorily stated in algebraic form.[4] But the old law of diminishing returns from land, properly qualified, remains valid as a special case.

Malthus was right in postulating a tendency for population, if unchecked, to increase at a "geometrical" rate. He was right in postulating a law of diminishing returns from land. But he was wrong in refusing (in his first edition) to recognize the possibilities of voluntary population restraint. He failed to foresee the possibilities of contraception by mechanical and chemical means. He was wrong, again, when he formulated his law of diminishing returns, in failing to recognize the enormous potential of technical progress.

So developments in the United States and Europe, in the century and three quarters since his book appeared, have made Malthus look in some respects like the worst prophet ever. Population in these "developed" countries has increased at an unparalleled rate, yet per capita economic welfare has also been advancing to levels once undreamed of. There are no signs that this rate of technical progress will diminish. Professor Dudley Kirk, of the Food Research Institute at Stanford University, insisted in 1968, for example, that "far from facing starvation, the world has the best food outlook in a generation."

4. Ludwig von Mises, *Human Action,* Henry Regnery, 1966 edition, pp. 127–31 and 341–50; Murray N. Rothbard, *Man, Economy, and State,* D. Van Nostrand, 1962, pp. 28–32, and Joseph A. Schumpeter, *History of Economic Analysis,* Oxford University Press, 1954, p. 587, and *passim.*

He attributed this to a new "green revolution," based on new seed grains and wider fertilizer use.

A New Hysteria

In spite of the serious errors in Malthus, we have witnessed in the last decade an outburst of "neo-Malthusianism," a new widespread fear, sometimes verging on hysteria, about a world "population explosion." Paul Erlich, professor of biology at Stanford University, in a book entitled *The Population Bomb,* warns us that we are all doomed if we do not control population growth. Professor Dennis Meadows of the Massachusetts Institute of Technology says:

"It used to take 1,500 years to double the world's population. Now it takes about 30 years. . . . Mankind is facing mass starvation, epidemics, uncontrollable pollution and wars if we don't discover new methods of population and industrial control and do it fast. If our society hasn't succeeded in ten years in coming to grips with these problems, I think it will be too late."[5]

Even the usual current estimates are almost as alarming. They run something like this: It was not until about 1830 that the world's population had reached a billion. By 1930 it had reached two billion. Now there are about three and a half billion. President Nixon estimated in 1970 that, at present rates of growth, world population will be seven billion at the end of the century and thereafter an additional billion will be added every five years or less.

Most of these predictions are reached by simply extrapolating recent annual growth rates and assuming that they will continue, come what may. When we look at the projections country by country, however, we find that the real problem is created by what is happening, not in Europe and in the United States, but in the so-called "underdeveloped" countries in Asia, Africa, and Latin America.

5. *National Enquirer,* May 16, 1971.

Based not on simple progression but on calculations of changing birth and death rates and other factors, the United Nations, in its *Bulletin of Statistics,* estimated in April, 1971, that Mainland China's population, assumed to have been 740 million in 1969, would rise to 1,165 million in the year 2000. India is expected to leap from 537 million in 1969 to 1,084 million in 2000. By the year 2000 UN statisticians estimate that the world population will reach 6,494 million—but 5,040 million will be in the less developed countries, and only 1,454 million in the more developed. In other words, the study foresees an average growth rate of only about 1 percent a year in the more developed countries, but of about 2.2 percent in the less developed countries—i.e., most of Asia, Africa, and Latin America.

This outlook is at least a partial vindication of Malthus. His central thesis, supported in the later editions of his *Essay* by a wealth of research, was that every advance in the arts of increasing subsistence had been absorbed in the past by a consequent increase of population, thus preventing any rise in the general level of living. He was right regarding the past; he is still right in his forecasts so far as most of the world is concerned. It is widely estimated that of the world's present three and a half billion people, nearly two billion are underfed. And it seems to be precisely where they are already underfed that they tend to multiply fastest, to the edge of subsistence.

Though the problem of population growth is most urgent in the backward countries, it exists everywhere. Those who are most concerned about overpopulation in the advanced countries today see it less as an immediate menace to the food supply than as a menace to "the quality of life." They foresee overcrowding, still bigger cities, more "urban sprawl," more automobiles, more roads, more traffic jams, more waste products, more garbage, more sewage, more smoke, more noxious fumes, and more pollutants, contaminants, and poisons.

Although these fears may be exaggerated, they have a rational basis. We may take it as a reasonable assumption that in most parts of the world today, even in the advanced countries, population has already reached or passed its optimum level in purely economic terms. In other words, there are very few places left in which it is probable that additional hands would lead to a more than proportionate increase in returns. The opposite is nearly everywhere more likely. Therefore we may assume that any increase in population will reduce per capita production, not necessarily in absolute amount, but in comparison with what it could be without a further population growth. From this standpoint the problem of overpopulation is not merely one for some distant future, even in the advanced countries, but one that exists now.

What, then, is the solution? Most of the neo-Malthusians, unfortunately, are collectivist in their thinking; they want to solve the problem *in the aggregate,* and by government coercion. They not only want governments to flood their countries with propaganda for The Pill, The Loop, and other methods of contraception, encouraging even abortion; they want to sterilize men and women. They demand "Zero Population Growth Now." A professor of "human ecology" at the University of California declares that the community cannot "watch children starve." Therefore: "If the community has the responsibility of keeping children alive it must also have the power to decide when they may be procreated. Only so can we save ourselves from the degradation of runaway population growth."[6]

The professor surely has the courage of his premises.

It is the great merit of Malthus to have been not only the first to see the problem clearly but also the first to propose the proper path to its solution. He was a relentless critic of the poor laws of his day:

"The poor laws of England tend to depress the general conditions of the poor. . . . Their first obvious tendency is to increase population without increasing the food for its support. A poor

6. Garrett Hardin in *The New York Times,* May 6, 1971.

man may marry with little or no prospect of being able to support a family without parish assistance. They may be said, therefore, to create the poor which they maintain. . . .

"If it be taught that all who are born have a *right* to support on the land, whatever be their number, and that there is no occasion to exercise any prudence in the affair of marriage so as to check this number, the temptations, according to all the known principles of human nature, will inevitably be yielded to, and more and more will gradually become dependent on parish assistance."[7]

Malthus's strictures did influence the Poor Law Reform of 1834. But no government in the world today is willing to accept his unpalatable conclusions. Nearly all continue to subsidize and reward indigent mothers or families in direct proportion to the number of children they bring into the world, legitimately or illegitimately, and cannot support.

Malthus was an individualist and a libertarian. His own proposed remedy for overpopulation was both voluntary and simple:

"I see no harm in drawing the picture of a society in which each individual is supposed strictly to fulfill his duties. . . . The happiness of the whole is to be the result of the happiness of individuals, and to begin first with them. No co-operation is required. Every step tells. He who performs his duty faithfully will reap the full fruits of it, whatever be the number of others who fail. This duty is intelligible to the humblest capacity. It is merely that he is not to bring beings into the world for whom he cannot find the means of support."[8]

If each of us adhered to this principle, no overpopulation problem would exist.

7. Malthus, *Essay on Population*, Book III, Ch. VI and VII.
8. *Ibid.*, Book IV, Ch. III.

CHAPTER 3

Defining Poverty

ANY STUDY OF POVERTY SHOULD LOGICALLY BEGIN WITH A DEFINITION of the problem we are trying to solve. Precisely what *is* poverty?

Of the thousands of books and articles on the subject that have appeared over the last two centuries, it is astonishing how few have troubled to ask this question. Their writers have taken it for granted that both they and their readers know precisely what is being discussed. Yet popularly the term is very vague. It is nearly always employed in a relative rather than an absolute sense. In Victorian England it became the fashion for some politicians to say that "the Rich and the Poor form Two Nations." But as every family's income, if arranged on a scale according to its dollar amount, would probably form a dot on a continuous smooth curve, the dividing line between the poor and the not-poor would be an arbitrary one. Is the poorer half of the population anywhere to be called the Poor, and the richer half the Rich?

The discussion today is conducted dominantly in these comparative terms. Our reformers are constantly telling us that we must improve the condition of the lowest fifth or the lowest third of the population. This way of discussing the subject was made fashionable by President Franklin D. Roosevelt in his Second Inaugural Address in January, 1937: "I see one third of a nation ill-housed, ill-clad, ill-nourished." (The objective standards on which this statement was based were never specified.)

It is obvious, however, that all merely relative definitions of poverty make the problem insoluble. If we were to double the real income of everybody, or multiply it tenfold, there would still be a lowest third, a lowest fifth, a lowest tenth.

Comparative definitions lead us, in fact, into endless difficulties. If poverty means being worse off than somebody else, then all but one of us is poor. An enormous number of us are, in fact, *subjectively* deprived. As one writer on poverty succinctly put it nearly sixty years ago: "It is part of man's nature never to be satisfied as long as he sees other people better off than himself."[1]

A discussion of the role that envy plays in economic and all human affairs can be deferred to another place. In any case we are driven to try to find an absolute or objective definition of poverty. This turns out to be more difficult than it might at first seem. Suppose we say that a man is in poverty when he has less than enough income, or less than enough in nutrition and shelter and clothing, to maintain himself in normal health and strength. We soon find that the objective determination of this amount is by no means simple.

Let us turn to some of the recent "official" definitions in the United States. In January, 1964, when President Johnson was launching his "war on poverty," the annual report of the Council of Economic Advisers contained a long section on the problem. This offered not one but several definitions of poverty. One

1. Hartley Withers, *Poverty and Waste,* London, Elder Smith, 1914; Second Revised Edition, John Murray, 1931, p. 4.

was relative: "One fifth of our families and nearly one fifth of our total population are poor." A second was at least partly subjective: "By the poor we mean those who are not now maintaining a decent standard of living—those whose basic needs exceed their means to satisfy them." Each of us might have his own conception of a "decent" standard, and every family might have its own ideas of its "needs." A third definition was: "Poverty is the inability to satisfy minimum needs."

The Council of Economic Advisers, basing its estimates on "low-cost" food budgets compiled by the Social Security Administration, decided that the poverty "boundary line" was established by "a family whose annual money income from all sources was $3,000 (before taxes and expressed in 1962 prices)." Yet on the very next page the Council report declared that in 1962 "5.4 million families, containing more than 17 million persons, had total incomes below $2,000." How could these 17 million persons exist and survive if they had so much less than enough "to satisfy minimum needs"?

In a 50-page study published in 1965,[2] Rose D. Friedman subjected these Council estimates to a thorough analysis. Using precisely the same data and the same concept of "nutritive adequacy" as the Council, she found that the dividing line between the poor and the not-poor would be not $3,000, but a figure around $2,200 as the relevant income for a nonfarm family of four. Where the Council on the basis of its figure estimated that 20 percent of all American families in 1962 were poor, Mrs. Friedman found that on her adjusted calculation only about 10 percent were poor.

I must refer the interested reader to the full text of her study for the details of her excellent analysis, but two of her disclosures will be enough to illustrate the carelessness of the Council's own estimates.

One astonishing error by the Council was to use its $3,000 a

2. *Poverty: Definition and Perspective.* American Enterprise Institute, Washington, D.C.

33

year estimate as the "poverty boundary" for all families of any size. Mrs. Friedman's estimates ranged from $1,295 for two-person households to $2,195 for four-person households to $3,-155 for households of seven persons or more. (The official "poverty line" estimates now also specify a similar range of differences for families of different sizes.)

A second error of the Council was equally astonishing. Based on a previous official estimate that a poor family of four needed about $1,000 a year in 1962 for adequate nutrition, the Council multiplied this amount arbitrarily by three to get what the family needed for all purposes. But it is notorious that poorer families have to spend a larger proportion of their income on food than do richer families. Mrs. Friedman found that this multiple of three was much higher than the level at which three fourths of the families concerned did get along on and still get an adequate diet. She found that the amount actually spent for food, on the average, by a family of four with an income of $2,200 was about $1,248 a year. In other words, the fraction of income spent on food at this level was about 60 percent and not 33 percent. Yet the official "poverty line" estimates, at this writing, are still kept unrealistically high by continuing to be implicitly based on this arbitrary multiple of three times adequate diet costs.

What Is "Adequate" Nutrition?

One of the great problems involved in arriving at any objective standard of poverty is the constantly changing concept of what constitutes "adequate" nutrition. This was once measured in calories. As time has gone on, and scientific research has continued, it has been insisted that adequacy also requires certain amounts of protein, calcium, iron, Vitamin A, thiamine, riboflavin, niacin, ascorbic acid, etc. The newest insistence has been on the need for a multitude of amino acids. Recently a nutrition survey done at Pennsylvania State College concluded that "only one person in a thousand escapes malnutrition!"[3] On this basis even affluence is no assurance of nutritional adequacy.

Yet compare this scientific ideal not only with the historic situation before the present century, when getting enough to eat was the major problem of the great majority of the populace of the world, but with the conditions that still prevail among that majority. Compared to a supposed subsistence minimum of 3,500 calories, half the people of the world today still get less than 2,250 calories per day, and live on a diet primarily of cereal in the form of millet, wheat, or rice. Another 20 percent get less than 2,750 calories per person per day. Only the well-to-do three tenths of the human race today get more than 2,750 calories as well as a varied diet which provides the calories that not only satisfy hunger but also maintain health.[4]

Official estimates of "poverty-threshold" income by Federal bureaus are still unrealistically high. I quote from a recent official bulletin:

"The decade of the sixties has witnessed a sizable reduction in the number of persons living in poverty. Since 1959, the first year for which data on poverty are available, there has been an average annual decline of 4.9 percent in the number of poor persons. However, between 1969 and 1970, the number of poor persons increased by about 1.2 million, or 5.1 percent. This is the first time that there has been a significant increase in the poverty population. In 1970, about 25.5 million persons, or 13 percent of the population, were below the poverty level, according to the results of the Current Population Survey conducted in March, 1971 by the Bureau of the Census."[5]

Yet though the estimate of the poor was then only 13 percent

3. Bulletin No. 1, July, 1968, Foundation for Nutrition and Stress Research, Redwood City, California.
4. Rose D. Friedman, *op. cit.*; M. K. Bennett, *The World's Food*, New York: Harper & Bros., 1954.
5. *Consumer Income*, Series P-60, No. 77, May 7, 1971, U.S. Department of Commerce, Bureau of the Census.

of the population compared with about 20 percent in 1962, the government statisticians were still using their old high estimate for 1962—and writing up the dollar amount year by year to correspond with increases in the Consumer Price Index. The same bulletin quoted above informs us: "The poverty threshold for a nonfarm family of four was $3,968 in 1970 and $2,973 in 1959." If Mrs. Friedman's more careful calculations had been used, the "poverty threshold" for a nonfarm family of four would have been closer to $2,900 than to $3,968 in 1970 and the percentage of "the poor" would have been closer to 7 percent than to 12.6. In fact, an earlier bulletin of the Bureau of the Census,[6] which had estimated that "about 1 out of 10 families were poor in 1969, compared with about 1 out of 5 in 1959," informs us that if the Bureau's various "poverty thresholds" for families of different sizes were decreased to 75 percent of its existing estimates (i.e., to approximately the levels suggested by Mrs. Friedman's calculations), then "the number of poor persons would drop by 40 percent in 1969, and the poverty rate for persons would drop from 12 percent to 7 percent."

It is clear from all this that government bureaucrats can make the numbers and percentage of "the poor," and hence the dimensions of the problem of poverty, almost whatever they wish, simply by shifting the definition.

And some of our American bureaucrats have been doing just that. On December 20, 1970, for example, the Bureau of Labor Statistics announced that, as of the spring of that year, it took a gross income of $12,134 to maintain a family of four on a "moderate" standard of living in the New York–northeastern New Jersey area. The implication was that any family of four with a smaller income than that was less than "moderately" well off and presumably the taxpayers should be forced to do something about it.

Yet the *median* income of a typical American family[7] was

6. Series P-60, No. 76, December 16, 1970.
7. Not necessarily a family of four. The term "family" as used by the Bureau

estimated by the Bureau of the Census to be only $9,433 in 1969. This means that half of the number of American families were receiving less than that. Clearly a good deal less than half of American families were lucky enough to be receiving the "moderate" income of $12,134.

Most of those who try to frame a definition of poverty no doubt have in mind some practical purpose to be served by such a definition. The purpose of the Federal bureaucracy is to suggest that any income below its definition constitutes a problem requiring government relief, presumably by taxing the families who earn higher incomes to supplement or subsidize the lower. If the present official U.S. definitions of poverty were applied to a country like India, we would have to label as poverty-stricken the overwhelming majority of its population. But we do not have to go to India for such an example. If we go back only a little more than forty years ago in our own country, we find that in the so-called prosperous year 1929 more than half of the people in the United States would have been labeled "poor" if the "poverty-threshold" income since developed by the Council of Economic Advisers had then been applied. (This is based on statistical comparisons that fully allow for the changes in the price level in the meantime.)[8]

Let us look at one more example of the consequences of establishing an excessive or merely relative definition of poverty.

"The term poverty may connote hunger, but this is not what is usually meant in discussions about poverty in America. Consider, for example, the facilities available to the poor. Tunica County, Mississippi, is the poorest county in our poorest state. About eight out of every ten families in this county had in-

for this calculation "refers to a group of two or more persons related by blood, marriage, or adoption and residing together; all such persons are considered members of the same family." *Economic Report of the President,* February, 1971, Table C-20, p. 220.

8. Source: Jeanette M. Fitzwilliams, "Size Distribution of Income in 1962," *Survey of Current Business,* April, 1963, Table 3; Herman P. Miller, *Rich Man-Poor Man,* New American Library, 1964, p. 47.

comes under $3,000 in 1960 [i.e., under the official "poverty-threshold" level] and most of them were poor by national standards; yet 52 percent owned television sets, 46 percent owned automobiles, and 37 percent owned washing machines. These families might have been deprived of hope and poor in spirit, but their material possessions, though low by American standards, would be the envy of the majority of mankind today.[9]

To sum up: It is difficult, and perhaps impossible, to frame a completely objective definition of poverty. Our conception of poverty necessarily involves a value judgment. People in different ages, in different countries, in different personal circumstances, will all have different ideas of what constitutes poverty, depending on the range of conditions to which they themselves are accustomed. But while the conception of poverty will necessarily be to some extent relative and even individual, we should make every effort to keep it as objective as we can. Otherwise if, for example, our national income in real terms continues to rise as much in the next forty years as in the past forty years, our social reformers will tend to raise correspondingly their standard of what constitutes "poverty." And if this happens, the paradoxical result will be that the problem of poverty will seem to them to be getting larger all the time when it is really getting smaller all the time.

One writer has seriously suggested that we "define as poor any family with an income less than one-half that of the median family."[10] But on this definition, if the wealth and income of all groups increased more or less proportionately, as in the past, and by no matter what rate or what multiple, the percentage of "the poor" would never go down, while the implied absolute amount of relief required would keep soaring.

Our definition obviously should not be such as to make our

9. Herman P. Miller, *Rich Man, Poor Man*, New York, Thomas Y. Crowell Co., 1971, pp. 110–111.

10. Victor R. Fuchs, "Toward a Theory of Poverty," in U.S. Chamber of Commerce, *The Concept of Poverty*, Washington, D.C., 1965, p. 74.

problem perpetual and insoluble. We must avoid any definition that implies the need of a level of help or any method of help that would tempt the recipient to become permanently dependent on it, and undermine his incentives to self-support. This is likely to happen whenever we offer an able-bodied adult in charity or relief more than or even as much as he could earn by working. What he needs is a level of subsistence sufficient to maintain reasonable health and strength. This subsistence level must constitute our working definition of the poverty line. Any relief program that tries to provide more than this for idle able-bodied adults will in the end do more harm than good to the whole community.

CHAPTER 4

The Distribution of Income

FOR MORE THAN A CENTURY SOCIALIST WRITERS HAVE LEVELED TWO main charges against capitalism: (1) It is not productive (or only wastefully productive, or far less productive than some imaginable socialist system would be); (2) It leads to a flagrantly unjust "distribution" of the wealth that it does produce; the workers are systematically exploited; "the rich get richer and the poor get poorer."

Let us consider these charges. That the capitalist system could ever have been accused of being unproductive, or of being very inefficiently productive, will seem incredible to most economic students of the present day, familiar with the record of the last generation; it will seem even more incredible to those familiar with the record since the middle of the eighteenth century. Yet the improvement in that early period remained hidden even from some astute contemporary observers. We have already seen how little the Malthus of 1798 (the date of the first edition of his *Essay on Population*) was aware of the productive transformation already achieved in the first half of the Industrial Revolution.

Yet much earlier, in 1776, Adam Smith had shown keen awareness of improvement: "The uniform, constant, and uninterrupted effort of every man to better his condition ... is frequently powerful enough to maintain the natural progress of things toward improvement, in spite of the extravagance of government, and of the greatest errors of administration."[1]

Smith rightly attributed this progress to the steady increase of capital brought about by private saving—to the "addition and improvement to those machines and instruments which facilitate and abridge labor."

"To form a right judgment" of this progress, he continued, "one must compare the state of the country at periods somewhat distant from one another [so as not to be deceived by short periods of recession]. ... The annual produce of the land and labor of England, for example, is certainly much greater than it was a little more than a century ago at the restoration of Charles II." And this again was certainly much greater "than we can suppose it to have been about a hundred years before, at the accession of Elizabeth."[2] Quite early in *The Wealth of Nations* we find Smith referring to the conditions of his own period as being comparatively, as a result of the increasing division of labor, a period of "universal opulence which extends itself to the lowest ranks of the people."[3]

If we leap ahead another century or more, we find the economist Alfred Marshall writing in the 1890s:

"The hope that poverty and ignorance may gradually be extinguished derives indeed much support from the steady progress of the working classes during the nineteenth century. The steam engine has relieved them of much exhausting and degrading toil; wages have risen; education has been improved and become more general. ... A great part of the artisans have ceased to belong to the 'lower classes' in the sense in which the

1. Adam Smith, *The Wealth of Nations*, Book II, Ch. III.
2. *Loc. cit.*
3. *Ibid.*, Book I, Ch. I.

term was originally used; and some of them lead a more refined and noble life than did the majority of the upper classes even a century ago."[4]

For more recent years we have the great advantage of getting beyond more or less impressionistic comparisons of economic progress to fairly reliable statistical comparisons. Our chief care here must be to avoid making such comparisons in terms of dollar income at current prices. Because of the continuous monetary inflation in the United States since the 1930s, this would give a very misleading impression. To get a true picture of the real improvement in production and welfare, in so far as these are measurable, allowance must be made for price increases. Statisticians do this by deflating recent prices and incomes in accordance with index numbers of average prices— in other words, by making their comparisons in terms of so-called "constant" dollars.

Let us begin with some overall figures. In the 59 years between 1910 and 1969 it is estimated that the real gross national product of the United States (the GNP) increased at an average rate of 3.1 percent a year compounded.[5] At such a rate the production of the country has been more than doubling every 24 years.

Let us see how this has looked expressed in billions of 1958 dollars:

Year	GNP
1929	$203.6
1939	209.4
1949	324.1
1959	475.9
1969	727.1

Source: Department of Commerce.

4. Alfred Marshall, *Principles of Economics,* 8th Ed., New York, Macmillan, pp. 3–4.
5. Based on estimates by the Department of Commerce expressed in "constant" (1958) dollars.

In the ten years from 1939 to 1949, then, the real gross national product of the country increased 55 percent; in the twenty years from 1939 to 1959 it increased 127 percent; in the thirty years from 1939 to 1969 it increased 242 percent.

If we now express this in terms of disposable per capita personal income (at 1958 prices) for these same years, the comparison is less striking because we are allowing for the growth in population, but the progress is still remarkable:

Year	Per Capita Income
1929	$1,236
1939	1,190
1949	1,547
1959	1,881
1969	2,517

Source: Department of Commerce.

In other words, disposable per capita personal income at constant prices increased 112 percent—more than doubled—in the generation from 1939 to 1969.

This disposes effectively of the charge that capitalism is unproductive, or unacceptably slow in increasing production. In the thirty years from 1939 to 1969 the United States was still the most capitalistic country in the world; and the world had never before witnessed anything comparable with this vast production of the necessities and amenities of life.

Gains Shared by the Masses

The foregoing figures do nothing, it is true, to answer the charge that capitalism distributes its gains unjustly—that it benefits only the already rich, and leaves the poor, at best, no better off than they were before. These charges are at least partly answered, however, as soon as we compare the *median* incomes of families in constant (1969) prices:

43

Year	Numbers (millions)	Median Income
1949	39.3	$4,779
1959	45.1	6,808
1969	51.2	9,433

Source: Department of Commerce.

As the *median* income means that there were just as many families earning more than the amount cited as those earning less, it follows that the 97 percent increase of median real incomes in this twenty-year period must have been shared in by the mass of the people. (The median incomes of "unrelated individuals," calculated on the same 1969 price basis, rose from $1,641 in 1949 to $2,931 in 1969.)

Other sets of figures confirm this conclusion. If we simply compare actual weekly wages paid in manufacturing, we find that these rose from $23.64 in 1939 to $129.51 in 1969—an increase of 448 percent. As the cost of living was constantly rising during this period, this of course greatly exaggerates labor's gains. Yet even after we restate these wages in terms of constant (1967) prices, we find the following changes in average gross weekly earnings:

Year	Wages (in 1967 prices)
1939	$56.83
1949	75.46
1959	101.10
1969	117.95

Source: Department of Labor.

So far from wages failing to keep pace with increases in living costs, real wages rose 108 percent in this thirty-year period.

Was the worker getting his "fair share," however, in the general increase in production—or was he getting a smaller share compared with, say, the owners of industry?

Let us begin by looking at the sources of personal income. Of the nation's total personal income of $801 billion in 1970, $570.5

44

billion, or 71 percent, was in wages and salaries and other labor income. Income from farming came to $16.2 billion, or 2 percent; business and professional income was $51.4 billion, or 6.4 percent. Rental income received by persons was $22.7 billion, or 2.8 percent; dividends came to $25.2 billion, or 3.1 percent; interest received by persons was $65.2 billion, or 8.1 percent. (Source: *Economic Indicators,* June, 1971, Council of Economic Advisers.) If we total these last three items we get $113.1 billion, or 14.1 percent, of "unearned" income. (The income from farming and from business was partly "earned" and partly "unearned," in undeterminable proportions.)

It is doubtful how much all this tells us about the distribution of income between the "rich" and the "poor." Total wage and salary disbursements include the salaries of highly paid executives and of television and motion-picture stars. On the other hand, rentals, dividends, and interest payments include many millions of moderate-sized individual sums that may represent the major part or the sole means of support of widows and orphans and persons too old or too ill to work. (There are some 30 million American stockholders, for example, and 25 million savings-bank accounts.)

A very significant figure, however, is the comparison of how much the employees get from the corporations with how much the owners get. Let us look first at a few facts about profits. In the five-year period from 1966 to 1970 inclusive, all manufacturing corporations of the United States earned profits after Federal income taxes of only 4.9 cents per dollar of sales. Manufacturing corporation profits after taxes as a percentage of stockholders' equity look a little better—they averaged 11.6 percent for the same five years. (Source: *Economic Report of the President,* January, 1972, p. 282.)

Both of these figures, however, overstate the real profits of the corporations. In a period of continuous inflation like the present, the corporations are forced by the tax laws to make inadequate deductions for depreciation of plant and equipment, based on original cost, and not sufficient to cover replacement costs. Profits as a percentage of equity are overstated for still another reason: they are stated in dollars of depreciated purchasing power compared with the dollars that were originally invested.

Lion's Share to Employees

What is more significant (and constantly forgotten) is that the employees of the corporations draw far more from them than the owners. This is exactly the opposite of what is commonly believed. Surveys by the Opinion Research Corporation have found that the median opinion of those polled was that the employees of American corporations receive only 25 cents out of each dollar available for division between the employees and the owners, and that the remaining 75 cents go to profits. The facts are quite the opposite. In 1970, for example, of the U.S. corporation income available for distribution between the workers and the owners, nine tenths went to the workers and only one tenth to the owners. Here is how, in billions of dollars, the division appeared over a series of years:

DIVISION OF U.S. CORPORATE INCOME BETWEEN
EMPLOYEES AND STOCKHOLDERS

	Profits After Tax	Percent for Profits	Percent for Payroll	Payrolls
1970	$36.4	9.0	91	$366.0
1969	40.0	10.2	89.8	350.5
1968	44.2	12.2	87.8	319.2
1967	43.0	12.8	87.2	291.8
1966	46.7	14.5	85.5	275.5
1960	24.8	11.6	88.4	188.8
1955	25.4	14.9	85.1	144.6

Derived from Office of Business Economics, U.S. Department of Commerce.

If we average out the five years from 1966 to 1970, we find that compensation to employees came to 88.2 percent of the corpora-

46

tion income available for division, and onl~
than an eighth, to profits available for s~

Suppose we look not at what was the~
the shareholders but at what they wer
years in dividends. In the five years fr~
averaged just about half of corporate pr~
pared with total payments to employees of $1,~
the period, total dividends came to $115.2 billions. ~
words, the corporation employees received almost fourtee~
times as much in pay as the shareowners received in dividends.

So if American workers are being "exploited" by the capitalists, it is certainly not evident on the face of the figures. One
important fact that the anticapitalist mentality so often forgets
is that corporation earnings do not constitute a common pool.
If manufacturing corporations earn an average of 12 percent
on their equity, it does not mean that every corporation earns
this average profit margin. Some will earn 20 percent on equity,
some 10 percent, some 3 percent—and many will suffer losses.
(Over a 40-year period an average of 45 percent of companies
—by number—reported losses annually. As a general rule,
small companies suffered losses more frequently than did the
large corporations.)

Another point to be kept in mind: When profits are large, it
does not mean that they are at the expense of the workers. The
opposite is more likely to be true. In 1932 and 1933, for example,
the two years when the nation's corporations as a whole
showed a net loss, the workers also suffered their worst years
from unemployment and wage cuts. In a competitive capitalistic economy, aggregate profits and aggregate wages tend to go
up and down together, with a slight lag for wages. And, of
course, when profits fall, unemployment rises. The following
table compares corporate profits before taxes with compensation of employees (both in billions of dollars), and with percentage of unemployment in ten selected years.

It is in the long-run interest of the workers as well as stock-

	Profits before Taxes	Compensation of Employees	Percentage Unemployment
	$10.5	$ 51.1	3.2
ɔ2	−1.3	31.1	23.6
ɔ33	−1.2	29.5	24.9
1940	9.8	52.1	14.6
1950	37.7	154.6	5.3
1960	49.9	294.2	5.5
1968	84.3	514.6	3.6
1969	78.6	565.5	3.5
1970	70.8	601.9	4.9
1971	81.0	641.9	5.9

Source: Department of Commerce.

holders for profits to be high. Ironically, union leaders are always complaining about "excessive" profits, and forgetting that wages and employment are directly dependent on the outlook for profits.

Turning from the sources of income, we come now to increases in family incomes over recent years and to the division of income between various segments of the population. Because of rising prices, comparisons between different years of family incomes in current dollars have little meaning. Here is a comparison, however, of the percent distribution of white families by income level, in constant (1968) dollars, between 1950 and 1968:

Families	1950	1968
Under $3,000	23.4%	8.9%
$3,000–4,999	26.8	11.0
$5,000–6,999	22.9	14.3
$7,000–9,999	16.6	24.0
$10,000–14,999 ⎫ $15,000 and over⎭	10.2	{ 26.1 { 15.7
Median income	$4,985	$8,936

Source: U.S. Department of Commerce, Bureau of the Census.

48

The sharp drop in the percentage of families with "constant" incomes under $3,000 is especially noteworthy. The rise in the overall "real" median income in this eighteen-year period was 79 percent.

A Look at Family Incomes

The percent of aggregate income received by each fifth of the number of families in the country and the percent of aggregate income received by the top 5 percent of families have changed much less over the years, but such change as has occurred has been toward a more equal distribution:

Families	1947	1960	1968
Lowest fifth	5.0%	4.9%	5.7%
Second fifth	11.8	12.0	12.4
Middle fifth	17.0	17.6	17.7
Fourth fifth	23.1	23.6	23.7
Highest fifth	43.0	42.0	40.6
Top 5 percent	17.2	16.8	14.0

Source: U.S. Department of Commerce, Bureau of the Census.

If the reader wishes to know how the various fifths of the population ranged in actual incomes in 1970, and in which fifth or bracket his own family income fell, he can learn it from the following table:

Rank of Family	Income Range	Percentage of Income Received
Lowest fifth	Under $5,100	6%
Second fifth	Between $5,100 and $8,400	12
Middle fifth	Between $8,400 and $11,400	18
Fourth fifth	Between $11,400 and $16,300	24
Highest fifth	$16,300 and over	41
Top 5 percent	$24,800 and over	14

Source: U.S. Department of Commerce, Bureau of the Census.

The income comparisons presented in this chapter fail to give any support whatever to the socialist contention that under a capitalist system the tendency is for the rich to get richer and for the poor to get poorer—or at any rate for the proportional "gap" between the rich and poor to increase. What the figures show, on the contrary, is that in a healthy, expanding capitalist economy the tendency is for both the rich and the poor to get richer more or less proportionately. If anything, the position of the poor tends to improve better than proportionately.

This becomes even clearer if, instead of merely comparing incomes in terms of dollars, we look at the comparative gains of the poor that have been brought about by the technological progress that has in turn to so large an extent been brought about by capitalism and capital accumulation. As Herman P. Miller has pointed out:

"Looking back, there is good reason to wonder why the 1920s were ever regarded as a golden age. . . . Take for example a simple matter like electric power. Today electricity in the home is taken for granted as a more or less inalienable right of every American. Practically every home—on the farm as well as in the city—is electrified. Even on southern farms, ninety-eight out of every hundred homes have electricity. In 1930, nine out of every ten farm homes were without this 'necessity.' And the country was much more rural than it is now.

"A more striking example is provided by the presence of a toilet in the home. . . . As recently as 1940, about 10 percent of city homes and 90 percent of farms lacked toilet facilities within the structure. This is not Russia or China that is being described, but these United States only thirty years ago."[6]

Even the sceptical Paul Samuelson conceded in 1961 that "the American income pyramid is becoming less unequal."[7]

6. Herman P. Miller, *Rich Man, Poor Man,* New York, Thomas Y. Crowell Co., 1971, pp. 44–45.
7. Paul Samuelson, *Economics: An Introductory Analysis,* 5th ed., New York, McGraw Hill Book Co., p. 114.

Amenities for the Masses

There can be little doubt that the technological progress of the last two generations has meant more to the families at the bottom of this pyramid than to those at the top. It is the overwhelming majority of Americans that now enjoy the advantages of running water, central heating, telephones, automobiles, refrigerators, washing machines, phonographs, radios, television sets—amenities that millionaires and kings did not enjoy a few generations ago.

Here are some of the figures of the percentage of American households owning cars and appliances in 1969:

	Cars (one or more)	Television black and white	color	Washing Machine	Refrigerator or freezer
All households	79.6%	79.0%	31.9%	70.0%	82.6%
Annual income					
under $3,000	44.7	77.5	9.5	49.8	75.0
$3,000–$3,999	67.0	83.5	16.9	60.9	76.8

Source: U.S. Department of Commerce, Bureau of the Census.

In view of the fact that government statisticians officially placed the "poverty threshold" for 1969 at $3,721 for a family of four, and $4,386 for a family of five, the percentage of families with incomes less than this owning cars and appliances is remarkable. In 1969, in addition, 90 percent of all American households had telephone service.

To these figures on the distribution of physical appliances we must add many intangibles. The most important of these is the enormous increase in the number of those who have enjoyed the advantage of an education. Broadly speaking, the percentage increase has been greatest for those at the bottom of the pyramid. A century ago (1870), only 57 percent of all children between 5 and 17 years of age attended school. By the turn of the century this had risen to 76 percent, by 1920 to 82 percent, and by 1960 to 89 percent. It was as low as this in 1960 only because children were starting school at 6 years of age instead of at 5. Nearly 97 percent of all children between 7 and 17 years of age were in school in 1960. Even more dramatic are the figures on schooling at a higher level. In 1870, only 2 percent of the relevant age group graduated from high school. This tripled to 6 percent by 1900, tripled again to 17 percent by 1920, and again to 50 percent by 1940. It had reached 62 percent by 1956. Enrollment in institutions of higher education—junior colleges, colleges, and universities—was less than 2 percent of the relevant age group in 1870, and more than 30 percent in 1960.[8]

Presenting the contrast in another way: Since 1910 the proportion of high school and college graduates has approximately doubled every thirty years. The percentage of adults who were high school graduates increased from 13.5 in 1910 to 24.1 in 1940 and to 54.0 in 1969. Comparable figures for college graduates in the same years were 2.7, 4.6, and 10.7 percent respectively. The proportion of adults with less than five years of school decreased at about the same rate that the graduates rose. The decline was from 23.8 percent in 1910 to 13.5 in 1940 and to 5.6 in 1969.[9]

We have seen that under a capitalist economy the tendency is for both rich and poor to become better off more or less proportionately, but that this economic progress has nevertheless meant more to those at the bottom of the income pyramid than to those at the top. These two results are not inconsistent. In a market economy, as overall productivity and real per capita incomes both increase, the production of each individual good or service is not increased proportionately, but that of

---

8. Author's source: Rose D. Friedman, *Poverty: Definition and Perspective,* Washington, American Enterprise Institute, 1965, p. 11.

9. *Digest of Educational Statistics;* 1970 ed. Office of Education, U.S. Department of Health, Education, and Welfare, p. 10.

the goods most urgently wanted by most people is increased most. This reflects the changes brought about by increased real income in individual marginal utilities. Even apart from the specific direction of technological progress, when everybody's real income doubles, say, the marginal satisfactions of those at the bottom of the income scale are increased more than the marginal satisfactions of those at the top. The latter merely buy more luxuries, or save more; the former can afford more necessities. Hence even a merely proportional increase in unequal incomes tends to reduce inequalities in real welfare. Or to put it another way, the proportional inequalities tend to mean less.

Pareto's Law

In 1896 the Italian economist Vilfredo Pareto, after a study of different countries for which statistics were then available, and also as between various periods of time, found that the statistics of inequality in the distribution of wealth showed a remarkable correspondence. As a result he framed what became celebrated as the Pareto Curve, or Pareto's Law. What he found was that the highest incomes were received by very few people, but from the highest to the lowest brackets of incomes there was a steady progression in the number of people who received them, and if the numbers in these different brackets were plotted they followed a remarkable and almost uniform curve. If the various levels of income and the number of persons in receipt of each level of income are represented graphically by logarithms, the "curve" so drawn is a straight line.

For the nonmathematical, Pareto also represented the distribution of wealth by a bell-shaped figure with concave sides, very broad at the base, for the large number receiving the lowest incomes, and very narrow at the top, for the small number receiving the highest incomes.

This "law" has been defended by many eminent statisticians and economists and attacked by many others. Carl Snyder declared, "the Pareto Curve is destined to take its place as one of the great generalizations of human knowledge."[10] A. C. Pigou was among those who criticized it.

Both defenders and critics have too often been influenced by emotional bias, and have tended to accept or reject the "law" in accordance with their political preconceptions. Social reformers have attacked it both because of its implication that incomes vary directly with the abilities of different individuals, and in proportion to those abilities. Pigou contended that there was no reason to suppose Pareto's law to represent a *necessary* distribution of income, and that to the extent that the "law" might be statistically valid it was so because "income depends, not on capacity alone, whether manual or mental, but on a combination of capacity and inherited property. Inherited property is not distributed in proportion to capacity, but is concentrated upon a small number of persons."[11]

Serving the Masses

Whatever the truth about Pareto's Law may be or may have been, the long-run historical tendency of capitalism has not only been to increase real incomes more or less proportionately nearly all along the line, but to benefit the masses even more than the rich. Before the Industrial Revolution the prevailing trades catered almost exclusively to the wants of the well-to-do. But mass production could succeed only by catering to the needs of the masses. And this could be done only by success in dramatically reducing the costs and prices of goods to bring them within the buying power of the masses. So modern capitalism benefited the masses in a double way—both by greatly increasing the wages of the masses of workers and greatly reducing the real prices they had to pay for what was produced.

10. Carl Snyder, *Capitalism the Creator,* New York, The Macmillan Co., 1940, p. 417.
11. A. C. Pigou, *The Economics of Welfare,* London, Macmillan, 4th ed., 1946, p. 651.

Under the feudal system, and nearly everywhere before the Industrial Revolution, a man's economic position was largely determined by the economic position of his parents. To what extent is this true in the United States of the present day? This is a difficult question to answer in quantitative terms, because one of the intangibles a man tends to "inherit" from his parents is his educational level, which so largely influences his adult earning power. But some of the partial answers we do have to this question are surprising. Herman P. Miller tells us:

"In 1968 fewer than one family out of a hundred in the top income group lived entirely on unearned income—interest, dividends, rents, royalties, and the like. The other ninety-nine did paid work or were self-employed in a business or profession. Nearly all of these families were headed by a man who worked at a full-time job. In 1968 over four-fifths of these men worked full time throughout the year."[12]

They also seemed to work longer hours than the average worker. Among the rich, also, "relatively few admit to having inherited a substantial proportion of their assets. Even among the very rich—those with assets of $500,000 or more—only one-third reported that they had inherited a substantial proportion of their assets; 39 percent claimed to have made it entirely on their own, and an additional 24 percent admitted to having inherited a small proportion of their assets."[13]

International Comparisons

I have said nothing so far of the comparison of American incomes with those of other nations. In absolute figures—in gross national product per capita, in ownership of passenger cars and TV sets, in use of telephones, in working time required to buy a meal—these comparisons have been all heavily in favor of the United States. In 1968, the per capita gross national

12. Miller, *op. cit.*, p. 150.
13. *Ibid.*, p. 157.

product of the country came to $4,379, compared with $3,315 in Sweden, $2,997 in Canada, $2,537 in France, $1,861 in the United Kingdom, $1,418 in Italy, $1,404 in Japan, $566 in Mexico, and $80 in India.[14]

More immediately relevant to the subject of this chapter is a comparison of the distribution of income in the United States with that in other countries. In this respect also the result has been largely in favor of the United States. A comparison of conditions in the 1950s made by Simon Kuznets found that the top 5 percent of families received 20 percent of the U.S. national income. Industrialized countries like Sweden, Denmark, and Great Britain showed approximately the same percentage. It was in the "underdeveloped" countries where the greatest internal disparities existed in incomes. For example, in El Salvador the top 5 percent of families received 36 percent of the national income, in Mexico 37 percent, in Colombia 42 percent. This comparison is one more evidence that capitalism and industrialization tend to reduce inequalities of income.

A Misleading Phrase

I have entitled this chapter "The Distribution of Income," and have been using that phrase throughout; but I have done so with reluctance. The phrase is misleading. It implies to many people that income is first produced, and *then* "distributed"—according to some arbitrary and probably unjust arrangement.

Something like this idea appears to have been in the back of the minds of the older economists who first began to arrange their textbooks under these headings. Thus Book I of John Stuart Mill's *Principles of Political Economy* (1848) is entitled "Production," and Book II, "Distribution." Mill wrote, at the beginning of this second book:

"The principles which have been set forth in the first part of

14. *Statistical Abstract of the United States*, 1970, p. 810.

this Treatise are, in certain respects, strongly distinguished from those on the consideration of which we are now about to enter. The laws and conditions of the production of wealth partake of the character of physical truths. There is nothing optional or arbitrary in them. . . .

"It is not so with the Distribution of Wealth. That is a matter of human institution solely. The things once there, mankind, individually or collectively, can do with them as they like. . . . The distribution of wealth, therefore, depends on the laws and customs of society."

This distinction, if not altogether false, is greatly overstated. Production in a great society could not take place—on the farms, in the extraction of raw materials, in the many stages of processing into finished goods, in transportation, marketing, saving, capital accumulation, guidance by price and cost and supply and demand—without the existence of security, law and order, and recognized property rights—the same rules and laws that enable each to keep the fruits of his labor or enterprise. Goods come on the market as the property of those who produced them. They are not first produced and then distributed, as they would be in some imagined socialist society. The "things" are not "once there." The period of production is never completed, to be followed by some separate period of distribution. At any given moment production is in all stages. In the automobile industry, for example, some material is being mined, some exists in the form of raw materials, some in finished or semifinished parts; some cars are going through the assembly line, some are on the factory lots awaiting shipment, some are in transport, some are in dealers' hands, some are being driven off by the ultimate buyers; most are in use, in various stages of depreciation and wear and need of replacement.

In brief, production, distribution, and consumption all go on continuously and concurrently. What is produced, and how much of it, and by what method, and by whom, depends at all times on the relative sums that those engaged in the process are receiving or expect to receive in profits or wages or other compensation. Production depends no less than distribution on "the laws and customs of society." If farmer Smith raises 100 bushels of potatoes and farmer Jones 200 bushels, and both sell them for the same price per bushel, Jones does not have twice as much income as Smith because it has been "distributed" to him. Each has got the market value of what he produced.

It would be better to speak of the *variation* between individual incomes than of their "distribution." I have used the latter term only because it is customary and therefore more readily understood. But it can be, to repeat, seriously misleading. It tends to lead to the prevalent idea that the solution to the problem of poverty consists in finding how to expropriate part of the income of those who have earned "more than they need" in order to "distribute" it to those who have not earned enough. The real solution to the problem of poverty, on the contrary, consists in finding how to increase the employment and earning power of the poor.

CHAPTER 5

The Story of Negr

percent in 1949
1969. Thus th
whites
riod

THE MYTH STILL ASSIDUOUSLY CULTIVATED IN SOME QUARTERS IS THAT the Negro community has been sunk in hopeless poverty and despair, because it has not been allowed to participate in the general economic prosperity of the last ten or twenty years. The actual record does not support this.

What we find, in fact, is that the Negroes as a whole have not only made great absolute economic gains in this period, but gains at least fully proportional to those made by the white population.

The median income of Negro families in 1949 (calculated in 1969 prices) was $2,538. In 1959 this had risen to $3,661, and in 1969 to $6,191. Thus the median income had risen 44 percent in the ten years from 1949 to 1959, and 144 percent in the twenty years to 1969. This was a real gain in "constant" dollars and therefore owed nothing to the steep rise in prices during the period. The percentage of Negro families with incomes under $3,000 (also calculated in constant 1969 dollars) fell from 58.1

o 41.9 percent in 1959 and to 20.4 percent in

Negroes not only shared proportionately with the
in the economic improvement of the twenty-year pe-
, but somewhat better than proportionately. Compared
ith the 144 percent increase in Negro family "real" incomes
between 1949 and 1969, white family real incomes in the same
period increased only 97 percent.[1]

I have presented the figures in this way in order to emphasize
the real economic progress made by the blacks in this twenty-
year period. But these figures standing by themselves could
give a misleading impression. They fail to call attention to the
big gap still remaining between the incomes of white and black
families. In 1949, when the median income of Negro families
was $2,538 (in 1969 prices) the median income of white fami-
lies was $4,973. In 1969, when the median income of black
families had risen to $6,191, that of white families had risen to
$9,794. Thus the median income of black families, which aver-
aged only 51 percent of that of white families in 1949, had
advanced to no more than 63 percent in 1969.

This, of course, is still far from satisfactory; but the comparison should not lead us to depreciate the extent of the blacks'
real gains. Some writers talk as if the only gain worth talking
about that the blacks have made is this gain in comparison
with increased white incomes. But this is a captious and confused way of looking at the matter, and leads to some paradoxical results. Suppose in this twenty-year period the gains of Negro families had been the same as they were in absolute terms,
but that the real incomes of white families had shown no improvement whatever. Then though only 20.4 percent of Negro
families would have had incomes under $3,000 in 1969, 23.4
percent of white families would still have had such low incomes, as they did in 1949. And though the median income of

1. Source: Department of Commerce, Bureau of the Census, *Economic Report of the President*, February, 1971, Table C-20, p. 220.

Negro families would have been $6,191 in 1969, the median income of white families (in 1969 prices) would have been only $4,973, as it was in 1949. In both respects the Negro families, though with no better incomes in absolute terms than they actually had in 1969, would have been better off than the white families. Could this be seriously regarded as a more desirable all-around situation?

In still other ways the Negro has made great progress in the last ten or twenty years. A leading example is in the field of education. In 1957, the median years of school completed by nonwhite men (who were eighteen years of age and over, and who were in the labor force) stood at 8.0 years; for white men the corresponding figure was 11.5 years, a gap of 3.5 years. By 1967, however, the median years of schooling for nonwhite men increased to 10.2 years, and for white men the figure had increased to 12.3 years, reducing the difference to 2.1 years.

One trouble with all the comparisons I have made so far is that, because they arbitrarily group all whites together on the one hand, and all blacks together on the other (for the sake of making overall comparisons), they may help to encourage the naive tendency of many people to think of the black community as a homogeneous, undifferentiated group all in the same circumstances and with the same outlook. But Negro leaders have reminded us, for example, that "Young Negroes are at least as hostile toward their elders as white New Leftists are toward their liberal parents."[2] In addition Negroes are separated by great gaps in experience—Northern from Southern, urban from rural—and great differences in income. In 1967, for example, the relative spread in incomes among the nonwhite population was even greater than among the whites. The lowest fifth of white families received 5.8 percent of the total income of such families, the highest fifth received 40.7 percent, and the top 5 percent of families 14.9 percent. But among non-

2. Bayard Rustin in *Harper's Magazine,* January, 1970.

white families, the lowest fifth received only 4.4 percent of the total income of such families, the highest fifth 44.7 percent, and the top 5 percent received 17.5 percent.

These differences are emphasized further when we compare selected groups of black families, from different regions, with the corresponding white groups. In 1969, for the nation as a whole, black families earned 61 percent as much as their white counterparts (compared with 54 percent in 1960). But in the North and West, black families overall earned 75 percent as much as white families. More striking, Northern black families with the husband and wife under age 35 both present, averaged an $8,900 annual income in 1969, or 91 percent of the average of their white counterparts, compared with only a 62 percent average in 1960. Still more striking, Northern black families with the husband and wife under age 24 averaged 107 percent of the income of their white counterparts. (The Census Bureau thinks this is probably the result of a sampling error. But that the income of such black families is at least equal to that of their white counterparts is suggested by the result of a similar sampling in 1968; this showed such black family incomes averaging 99 percent of corresponding white incomes.)

It is significant that where we find the Negroes making the least progress comparatively is in the areas where the free market is not allowed to operate. This is particularly striking in labor union membership. In the unionized trades the unwritten rule seems to be that the higher the pay, the harder it is for blacks to get in. They make up 11 percent of the labor force. But at latest count, in such high-paying trades as plumbers, sheet-metal workers, electrical workers, and elevator constructors, less than 1 percent of the workers are black.[3]

In one important respect, the position of the Negroes has retrogressed. An increasing gap has developed between the respective rates of unemployment of white and blacks. In July,

3. Author's source: *Time,* April 6, 1970.

1972, the overall rate of unemployment among whites was 5.0 percent, among Negroes 9.9 percent. A difference of this sort has long existed. For example, even in the relatively good employment years 1950 to 1954 inclusive, when the white unemployment rate averaged 3.7 percent, the rate for Negroes averaged 6.8 percent. Part of this difference probably reflected discrimination by employers, and part of it the exclusion of Negroes from unions. In those five years unemployment among teenagers (16 to 19) was also higher, as it is now, than in the working force as a whole. But the gap in this respect between white and black teenagers was comparatively small. Unemployment among white teenagers in 1950 to 1954 averaged 10.3 percent, and among black teenagers 11.1 percent. Since that time the situation has been steadily deteriorating. In June, 1971, the unemployment rate among white teenagers was 13.5 percent, while among black teenagers it reached the appalling level of 33.8 percent.

Harm of Minimum Wage Laws

By far the main cause of this has been the Federal minimum wage law. Minimum wage legislation has been on the books since 1938, but in March 1956 the minimum rate was jacked up from 75 cents to $1 an hour, and it has since been raised by successive jumps to $1.60 an hour in February, 1968. But the law cannot make a worker worth a given amount by making it illegal for anyone to offer him less. It can merely make it unprofitable for employers to hire workers of low skills, and therefore forces such workers into unemployment. One of the greatest helps we could give the Negro today would be to repeal the statutory minimum wage.

What our politicians still do not realize is that the greatest counteracting force to racial discrimination is the free market. As the economist W. H. Hutt has put it, "The market is color-blind." If an employer can make a greater profit by employing

63

a Negro than a white man at a given job, he is likely to do it. Even the militant Negro Marcus Garvey recognized this, though in a somewhat cynical manner:

"It seems strange and a paradox, but the only convenient friend the Negro worker or laborer has in America at the present time is the white capitalist. The capitalist being selfish— seeking only the largest profit out of labor—is willing and glad to use Negro labor wherever possible on a scale reasonably below the standard union wage . . . but if the Negro unionizes himself to the level of the white worker, the choice and preference of employment is given to the white worker."[4]

In a free market, however, Negro employment does not necessarily depend on acceptance of a lower wage rate. If a Negro—say an outstanding professional baseball player or musician—is clearly superior to the best white competitor, he is likely to be employed in preference, at an even higher rate, because the employer expects to make a greater profit on him.

The chief hope for the economic progress of the Negroes lies not in some dream-world effort to form a separate "black economy," but in their becoming and being accepted as a more fully integrated part of a great expanding capitalist economy. In spite of the discrimination that still exists, the economic position of the Negro in the United States is not only incomparably higher than in Haiti or in any of the all-black countries of Africa, but higher than most whites even in the industrialized countries of Europe.

For what the best available statistical comparisons are worth, here they are: As compared with a median annual income of $2,138 for Negro unrelated individuals in 1968, the per capita gross national product for that year was $91 in Haiti, $238 in Ghana, $298 in Zambia, and $304 in the Ivory Coast. In Chad, the Congo, Mali, Niger, and Nigeria, it ranged from a low of $63 to a high of $88.[5]

---

4. Quoted by Bayard Rustin, *Harper's Magazine,* January, 1970.
5. Source: *Statistical Abstract,* 1970, p. 810.

Turning to European comparisons: In the early 1960's, when it was calculated that some 44 percent of America's nonwhite population was below the so-called poverty line of $3,000 a year, it developed that some 75 percent of Britain's entire, predominantly white, population was also below that line.[6] The $2,138 median income for American unrelated Negroes in 1968 compares (for whatever such a comparison is worth) with a per capita gross national product for that year of $1,544 in Austria, $2,154 in Belgium, $2,206 in West Germany, $1,418 in Italy, and $1,861 in the United Kingdom.

What chiefly counts is the productivity of the whole economy; what counts is the maximization of the incentives to that productivity. And those incentives are maximized when opportunities are maximized; when we neither favor nor discriminate against any man because of his color, but treat everyone according to his merits as an individual.

6. Edmund K. Faltermayer, *Fortune*, March, 1964.

CHAPTER 6

Poor Relief in Ancient Rome

INSTANCES OF GOVERNMENT RELIEF TO THE POOR CAN BE FOUND FROM the earliest times. Though the records are vague in important particulars, we do know a good deal about what happened in ancient Rome. A study of that case may enable us to draw a few lessons for our own day.

Roman "social reform" appears to have begun in the period of the Republic, under the rule of the Gracchi. Tiberius Gracchus (c. 163–133 B.C.) brought forward an agrarian law providing that no person should own more than 500 jugera of land (about 300 acres), except the father of two sons, who might hold an additional 250 jugera for each. At about the same time that this bill was passed, Attalus III of Pergamum bequeathed his kingdom and all his property to the Roman people. On the proposal of Gracchus, part of this legacy was divided among the poor, to help them buy farm implements and the like. The new agrarian law was popular, and even survived Tiberius's public assassination.

He was succeeded by his younger brother Gaius Gracchus (158–122 B. C.). In the ancient world transport difficulties were responsible for famines and for wild fluctuations in wheat prices. Among the reforms that Gaius proposed was that the government procure an adequate supply of wheat to be sold at a low and fixed price to everyone who was willing to stand in line for his allotment once a month at one of the public granaries that Gaius had ordered to be built. The wheat was sold below the normal price—historians have rather generally guessed at about half-price.

The record is not clear concerning precisely who paid for this generosity, but the burden was apparently shifted as time went on. Part of the cost seems to have been borne by Rome's richer citizens, more of it seems to have been raised by taxes levied in kind on the provinces, or by forced sales to the State at the lower prices, or eventually by outright seizures.

Though Gaius Gracchus met a fate similar to his brother's—he was slain in a riot with 3,000 of his followers—"the custom of feeding the Roman mob at the cost of the provinces," as the historian M. Rostovtzeff sums it up, "survived not only Gracchus but the Republic itself; though," as he adds ironically, "perhaps Gracchus himself looked upon the law as a temporary weapon in the strife, which would secure him the support of the lower classes, his main source of strength."[1]

An excellent account of the subsequent history of the grain dole can be found in H. J. Haskell's book *The New Deal in Old Rome* (New York, Knopf, 1939). I summarize this history here:

There was no means test. Anyone willing to stand in the bread line could take advantage of the low prices. Perhaps 50,000 applied at first but the number kept increasing. The senate, although it had been responsible for the death of Gaius Gracchus, did not dare abolish the sale of cheap wheat. A conservative government under Sulla did withdraw the cheap

1. M. Rostovtzeff, *History of the Ancient World,* Oxford, Clarendon Press, Vol. 2, p. 112.

wheat, but shortly afterward, in a period of great unrest, restored it, and 200,000 persons appeared as purchasers. Then a politician named Claudius ran for tribune on a free-wheat platform, and won.

A decade later, when Julius Caesar came to power, he found 320,000 persons on grain relief. He succeeded in having the relief rolls cut to 150,000 by applying a means test. After his death the rolls climbed once again to 320,000. Augustus once more introduced a means test and reduced the number to 200,000.

Thereafter during the Imperial prosperity the numbers on relief continued at about this figure. Nearly 300 years later, under the Emperor Aurelian, the dole was extended and made hereditary. Two pounds of bread were issued to all registered citizens who applied. In addition pork, olive oil, and salt were distributed free at regular intervals. When Constantinople was founded, the right to relief was attached to new houses in order to encourage building.

The political lesson was plain. Mass relief, once granted, created a political pressure group that nobody dared to oppose. The long-run tendency of relief was to grow and grow. Rostovtzeff explains how the process worked:

"The administration of the city of Rome was a heavy burden on the Roman state. Besides the necessity of making Rome a beautiful city, worthy of its position as the capital of the world ... there was the enormous expense of feeding and amusing the population of Rome. The hundreds of thousands of Roman citizens who lived in Rome cared little for political rights. They readily acquiesced in the gradual reduction of the popular assembly under Augustus to a pure formality, they offered no protest when Tiberius suppressed even this formality, but they insisted on their right, acquired during the civil war, to be fed and amused by the government.

"None of the emperors, not even Caesar or Augustus, dared to encroach on this sacred right of the Roman proletariate.

They limited themselves to reducing and fixing the numbers of the participants in the distribution of corn and to organizing an efficient system of distribution. They fixed also the number of days on which the population of Rome was entitled to a good spectacle in the theatres, circuses, and amphitheatres. But they never attacked the institution itself. Not that they were afraid of the Roman rabble; they had at hand their praetorian guard to quell any rebellion that might arise. But they preferred to keep the population of Rome in good humour. By having among the Roman citizens a large group of privileged pensioners of the state numbering about 200,000 men, members of the ancient Roman tribes, the emperors secured for themselves an enthusiastic reception on the days when they appeared among the crowd celebrating a triumph, performing sacrifices, presiding over the circus races or over the gladiatorial games. From time to time, however, it was necessary to have a specially enthusiastic reception, and for this purpose they organized extraordinary shows, supplementary largesses of corn and money, banquets for hundreds of thousands, and distributions of various articles. By such devices the population was kept in good temper and the 'public opinion' of the city of Rome was 'organized.' "[2]

The decline and fall of the Roman Empire has been attributed by historians to a bewildering variety of causes, from the rise of Christianity to luxurious living. We must avoid any temptation to attribute all of it to the dole. There were too many other factors at work—among them, most notably, the institution of slavery. The Roman armies freely made slaves of the peoples they conquered. The economy was at length based on slave labor. Estimates of the slave population in Rome itself range all the way from one in five to three to one in the period between the conquest of Greece (146 B.C.) and the reign of Alexander Severus (A.D. 222–235).

2. M. Rostovtzeff, *The Social and Economic History of the Roman Empire*, Oxford, Clarendon Press, 2nd ed., 1957, pp. 81–2.

The abundance of slaves created great and continuing unemployment. It checked the demand for free labor and for labor-saving devices. Independent farmers could not compete with the big slave-operated estates. In practically all productive lines, slave competition kept wages close to the subsistence level.

Yet the dole became an integral part of the whole complex of economic causes that brought the eventual collapse of Roman civilization. It undermined the old Roman virtue of self-reliance. It schooled people to expect something for nothing. "The creation of new cities," writes Rostovtzeff, "meant the creation of new hives of drones." The necessity of feeding the soldiers and the idlers in the cities led to strangling and destructive taxation. Because of the lethargy of slaves and undernourished free workmen, industrial progress ceased.

There were periodic exactions from the rich and frequent confiscations of property. The better-off inhabitants of the towns were forced to provide food, lodging, and transport for the troops. Soldiers were allowed to loot the districts through which they passed. Production was everywhere discouraged and in some places brought to a halt.

Ruinous taxation eventually destroyed the sources of revenue. It could no longer cover the State's huge expenditures, and a raging inflation set in. There are no consumer price indexes by which we can measure this, but we can get some rough notion from the price of wheat in Egypt. This was surprisingly steady, Rostovtzeff tells us, in the first and second centuries, especially in the second: it amounted to 7 or 8 drachmas for one *artaba* (about a bushel). In the difficult times at the end of the second century it was 17 or 18 drachmas, almost a famine price, and in the first half of the third it varied between 12 and 20 drachmas. The depreciation of money and the rise in prices continued, with the result that in the time of the Emperor Diocletian one *artaba* cost 120,000 drachmas. This means that the price was about 15,000 times as high as in the second century.

In 301 Diocletian compounded the evil by his price-fixing edict, which punished evasion with death. Out of fear, nothing was offered for sale and the scarcity grew much worse. After a dozen years and many executions, the law was repealed.

The growing burden of the dole was obviously responsible for a great part of this chain of evils, and at least two lessons can be drawn. The first, which we meet again and again in history, is that once the dole or similar relief programs are introduced, they seem almost inevitably—unless surrounded by the most rigid restrictions—to get out of hand. The second lesson is that once this happens the poor become more numerous and worse off than they were before, not only because they have lost self-reliance, but because the sources of wealth and production on which they depended for either doles or jobs are diminished or destroyed.

CHAPTER 7

The Poor Laws of England

ONE WOULD GET THE IMPRESSION, READING MOST OF THE DISCUSSIONS in today's American newspapers and magazines, that no one had ever thought of doing anything for the poor until Franklin Roosevelt's New Deal in the 1930s, or even until President Johnson's War on Poverty in the 1960s. Yet private charity is as old as mankind; and the history of governmental poor relief, even if we ignore the ancient world, can be traced back more than four centuries.

In England the first poor law was enacted in 1536. In 1547 the city of London levied compulsory taxes for the support of the poor. In 1572, under Elizabeth, a compulsory rate was imposed on a national scale. In 1576 the compulsion was imposed on local authorities to provide raw materials to give work to the unemployed. The Statute of 1601 compelled the Overseers of the Poor in every parish to buy "a convenient stock of flax, hemp, wool, thread, iron and other stuff to set the poor to work."

It was not compassion alone, or perhaps even mainly, that led to these enactments. During the reign of Henry VIII bands of "sturdy beggars" were robbing and terrorizing the countryside, and it was hoped that relief or the provision of work would mitigate this evil.

Poor relief, once started, kept growing. According to the early statistician Gregory King (1648–1712), toward the end of the seventeenth century over one million persons, nearly a fifth of the whole English nation, were in occasional receipt of alms, mostly in the form of public relief paid by the parish. The poor rate was a charge of nearly £800,000 a year on the country and rose to a million in the reign of Anne.

"There was seldom any shame felt in receiving outdoor relief, and it was said to be given with a mischievous profusion. Richard Dunning declared that in 1698 the parish dole was often three times as much as a common laborer, having to maintain a wife and three children, could afford to expend upon himself; and that persons once receiving outdoor relief refuse ever to work, and 'seldom drink other than the strongest alehouse beer, or eat any bread save what is made of the finest wheat flour.' The statement must be received with caution, but such was the nature of the complaint of some rate-payers and employers about the poor law."[1]

In 1795 a momentous step was taken that enormously aggravated the whole relief problem. The justices of Berkshire, meeting at Speenhamland, decided that wages below what they considered an absolute minimum should be supplemented by the parish in accordance with the price of bread and the number of dependents a man had. Their decision received Parliamentary confirmation the next year. In the succeeding thirty-five years this system (apparently the first "guaranteed minimum income") brought a train of evils.

The most obvious to the taxpayers was a geometric rise in the cost of relief. In 1785 the total cost of poor law administration

1. G. M. Trevelyan, *English Social History,* David McKay, 1942, p. 278.

was a little less than £2 million; by 1803 it had increased to a little more than £4 million; and by 1817 it had reached almost £8 million. This final figure was about one sixth of total public expenditure. Some parishes were particularly hard hit. One Buckinghamshire village reported in 1832 that its expenditure on poor relief was eight times what it had been in 1795 and more than the rental of the whole parish had been in that year.[2] One village, Cholesbury, became bankrupt altogether, and others were within measureable distance of it.

But even the public expense was not the worst of the evil. Much greater was the increasing demoralization of labor, culminating in the riots and fires of 1830 and 1831.

It was in the face of this situation that the Whig government decided to intervene. In 1832 a royal commission was appointed to inquire into the whole system. It sat for two years. The report and recommendations it brought in became the basis of the reforms adopted in Parliament by a heavy majority (319 to 20 on the second reading) and embodied in the Poor Law Amendment Act of 1834.

The report was signed by the nine commissioners. The secretary was Edwin Chadwick; one of the commissioners was the eminent economist Nassau W. Senior. The text of the report itself ran to 362 pages; together with its appendices it came to several bulky volumes. It was widely regarded as a "masterly example of a thorough, comprehensive, and unbiased inquiry." As late as 1906, one British writer, W. A. Bailward, described it as a "Blue-book which, as a study of social conditions, has become a classic."[3]

But today the report is just as if it had never existed. Schemes are being proposed on all sides, which their sponsors assume to be brilliantly original, but which would restore the very relief and income-guarantee systems that failed so miserably in the

2. "Poor Law," *Encyclopedia Britannica,* 1965.
3. J. St. Loe Strachey, ed., *The Manfacture of Paupers,* London, John Murray, 1907, p. 108.

74

late eighteenth and early nineteenth centuries, and which the report of 1834 so devastatingly analyzed.

The Speenhamland plan, and schemes like it, endeavored to insure that people were paid, not in accordance with the going rate of wages, or the market value of their services, but in accordance with their "needs," based on the size of their families. A married man was paid more than a single man, and paid still more on a scale upward in accordance with the number of his children. The government—i.e., the taxpayers—paid the difference between his market rate of wages and this scale of minimums.

One effect, of course, was to depress the market rate of wages, because the employer found he could reduce the wages he offered and let the taxpayers make up the deficiency. It made no difference to the worker himself who paid him how much of the fixed total that he got. Another effect was to demoralize the efficiency of labor, because a man was paid in accordance with the size of his family and not in accordance with the worth of his efforts. The average unskilled laborer had nothing to gain by improving his efforts and efficiency, and nothing to lose by relaxing them.

The Commission Report of 1832

But let us turn to the text of the Commission's report, and let the following excerpts speak for themselves. They are taken almost at random:

"The laborer under the existing system need not bestir himself to seek work; he need not study to please his master; he need not put any restraint upon his temper; he need not ask relief as a favor. He has all a slave's security for subsistence, without his liability to punishment. As a single man, indeed, his income does not exceed a bare subsistence; but he has only to marry, and it increases. Even then it is unequal to the support of a family; but it rises on the birth of each child. If his family is numerous, the parish becomes his principal paymaster; but small as the usual allowance of 2s. a head may be, yet when there are more than three children, it generally exceeds the average wages given in a pauperized district. A man with a wife and six children, entitled, according to the scale, to have his wages made up to 16s. a week, in a parish where the wages paid by individuals do not exceed 10s. or 12s., is almost an irresponsible being. All the other classes of society are exposed to the vicissitudes of hope and fear; he alone has nothing to lose or to gain. . . .

"The answer given by the magistrates, when a man's conduct is urged by the overseer against his relief, is: 'We cannot help that; his wife and family are not to suffer because the man has done wrong. . . .'

"Too frequently petty thieving, drunkenness, or impertinence to a master, throw able-bodied laborers, perhaps with large families, on the parish funds, when relief is demanded as a right, and if refused, enforced by a magistrate's order, without reference to the cause which produced his distress, viz., his own misconduct, which remains as a barrier to his obtaining any fresh situation, and leaves him a dead weight upon the honesty and industry of his parish. . . .

"It appears to the pauper that the government has undertaken to repeal, in his favor, the ordinary laws of nature; to enact that the children shall not suffer from the misconduct of their parents—the wife for that of the husband, or the husband for that of the wife: that no one shall lose the means of comfortable subsistence, whatever be his indolence, prodigality, or vice: in short, that the penalty which, after all, must be paid by some one for idleness and improvidence, is to fall, not on the guilty person or on his family, but on the proprietors of the lands and houses encumbered by his settlement. . . .

" 'In the rape of Hastings,' says Mr. Majendie, 'the assistant overseers are reluctant to make complaints for neglect of work, lest they should become marked men and their lives rendered uncomfortable or even unsafe. Farmers permit their laborers to receive relief, founded on a calculation of a rate of wages lower than that actually paid: they are unwilling to put themselves in collision with the laborers, and will not give an account of earnings, or if they do, beg that their names not be mentioned. . . . Farmers are afraid to express their opinions against a pauper who applies for relief, for fear their premises should be set fire to. . . .

" 'In Brede, the rates continue at an enormous amount. The overseer says much of the relief is altogether unnecessary; but he is convinced that if an abatement was attempted, his life would not be safe.' . . . 'I found in Cambridgeshire,' says Mr. Power, 'that the apprehension of this dreadful and easily perpetrated mischief [fire] has very generally affected the minds of the rural parish officers of this country, making the power of the paupers over the funds provided for their relief almost absolute, as regards any discretion on the part of the overseer.' . . .

"Mr. Thorn, assistant overseer of the parish of Saint Giles, Cripplegate, London, says:

" 'The out-door relief [i.e., relief given outside of a poorhouse] in the city of London would require almost one man to look after every half dozen of able-bodied men, and then he would only succeed imperfectly in preventing fraud. They cheat us on all hands. . . .

" 'By far the greater proportion of our new paupers are persons brought upon the parish by habits of intemperence. . . . After relief has been received at our board, a great portion of them proceed with the money to the palaces of gin-shops, which abound in the neighborhood. However diligent an assistant overseer, or an officer for inquiry, may be, there are numerous cases which will baffle his utmost diligence and sagacity. . . .

" 'It is the study of bad paupers to deceive you all they can, and as they study their own cases more than any inquirer can study each of the whole mass of different cases which he has to inquire into, they are sure to be successful in a great many instances. The only protection for the parish is to make the parish the hardest task-master and the worst paymaster that can be applied to.' "

To economize space, my remaining quotations from the Commissioners' criticisms of the conditions they found must be few and brief.

In many parishes, "the pressure of the poor-rate [i.e., taxes on property] has reduced the rent to half, or to less than half, of what it would have been if the land had been situated in an unpauperized district, and some in which it has been impossible for the owner to find a tenant. . . .

"Says Mr. Cowell: 'The acquaintance I had with the practical operation of the Poor Laws led me to suppose that the pressure of the sum annually raised upon the rate-payers, and its progressive increase, constituted the main inconvenience of the Poor Law system. The experience of a few weeks served to convince me that this evil, however great, sinks into insignificance when compared with the dreadful effects which the system produces on the morals and happiness of the lower orders. . . ."

The relief system was found to encourage "bastardy." "To the woman, a single illegitimate child is seldom any expense, and two or three are a source of positive profit. . . . The money she receives is more than sufficient to repay her for the loss her misconduct has occasioned her, and it really becomes a source of emolument. . . .

"The sum allowed to the mother of a bastard is generally greater than that given to the mother of a legitimate child; indeed the whole treatment of the former is a direct encouragement to vice. . . .

" 'Witness mentioned a case within his own personal cognizance, of a young woman of four-and-twenty, with four bastard children; she is receiving 1s. 6d. weekly for each of them. She told him herself, that *if she had one more she should be very comfortable.* Witness added, "They don't in reality keep the children; they let them run wild, and enjoy themselves with the money.' "

Given a modernization of phraseology and an appropriate change in the monetary amounts mentioned, this description of relief conditions and consequences in the early years of the nineteenth century could easily pass as a description of such conditions in, say, New York City in 1972.

What, then, in the face of these results of the prior Poor Law, were the recommendations of the commission? It desired to assure "that no one need perish from want"; but at the same time it suggested imposing conditions to prevent the abuse of this assurance.

"It may be assumed, that in the administration of relief, the public is warranted in imposing such conditions on the individual relieved as are conducive to the benefit either of the individual himself, or of the country at large, at whose expense he is to be relieved.

"The first and most essential of all conditions . . . is that his situation on the whole shall not be made really or apparently so eligible [i.e., desirable] as the situation of the independent laborer of the lowest class. Throughout the evidence it is shown, that in proportion as the condition of any pauper class is elevated above the condition of independent laborers, the condition of the independent class is depressed; their industry is impaired, their employment becomes unsteady, and its remuneration in wages is diminished. Such persons, therefore, are under the strongest inducements to quit the less eligible class of laborers and enter the more eligible class of paupers. . . . Every penny bestowed, that tends to render the condition of the pauper more eligible than that of the independent laborer, is a bounty on indolence and vice. . . .

"We do not believe that a country in which . . . every man, whatever his conduct or his character [is] ensured a *comfort-*

79

able subsistence, can retain its prosperity, or even its civilization.

"The main principle of a good Poor-Law administration [is] the restoration of the pauper to a position below that of the independent laborer."

The report then followed with its detailed recommendations, which involved many administrative complexities.

Nassau Senior's Defense

In 1841, seven years after the enactment of the new Poor Law, when a whole series of amendments was being proposed to it by various members of Parliament, Nassau Senior, in an anonymous pamphlet signed merely "A Guardian," came to the defense of the original act, and explained its rationale perhaps in some ways better than did the original report.

"In the first place," he wrote, "it was necessary to get rid of the allowance system—the system under which relief and wages were blended into one sum, the laborer was left without motive to industry, frugality, or good conduct, and the employer was forced, by the competition of those around him, to reduce the wages which came exclusely from his own pocket, and increase the allowance to which his neighbors contributed.

"Supposing this deep and widely extended evil to be extirpated, and the poorer classes to be divided into two marked portions—independent laborers supported by wages and paupers supported by relief—there appeared to be only three modes by which the situation of the pauper could be rendered the less attractive.

"First, by giving to the pauper an inferior supply of the necessaries of life, by giving him worse food, worse clothing, and worse lodging than he could have obtained from the average wages of his labor. . . .

"A second mode is to require from the applicant for relief, toil more severe or more irksome than that endured by the independent laborer. . . .

"The third mode is, to a certain degree, a combination of the two others, avoiding their defects. It is to require the man who demands to be supported by the industry and frugality of others to enter an abode provided for him by the public, where all the necessaries of life are amply provided, but excitement and mere amusement are excluded—an abode where he is better lodged, better clothed, and more healthily fed than he would be in his own cottage, but is deprived of beer, tobacco, and spirits —is forced to submit to habits of order and cleanliness—is separated from his usual associates and his usual pastimes, and is subject to labor, monotonous and uninteresting. This is the workhouse system."

The Royal Commission, in defending that system, had argued that even if "relief in a well-regulated workhouse" might be, "in some rare cases, a hardship, it appears from the evidence that it is a hardship to which the good of society requires the applicant to submit. The express or implied ground of his application is, that he is in danger of perishing from want. Requesting to be rescued from that danger out of the property of others, he must accept assistance on the terms, whatever they may be, which the common welfare requires. The bane of all pauper legislation has been the legislation for extreme cases. Every exception, every violation of the general rule to meet a real case of unusual hardship, lets in a whole class of fraudulent cases, by which that rule must in time be destroyed. Where cases of real hardship occur, the remedy must be applied by individual charity, a virtue for which no system of compulsory relief can be or ought to be a substitute."

The Dilemma of Relief

To later generations the reforms introduced by the Poor Law Amendments of 1834 came to seem needlessly harsh and even heartless. But the Poor Law Commissioners did courageously try to face up to a two-sided problem that the generation before them had ignored and many of the present generation seem once more to ignore—"the difficult problem," as Nassau Senior put it, "how to afford to the poorer classes adequate relief without material injury to their diligence or their providence." In his 1841 pamphlet we find him rebuking "the persons who would legislate for extreme cases—who would rather encourage any amount of debauchery, idleness, improvidence, or imposture, than suffer a single applicant to be relieved in a manner which they think harsh. . . . [They] would reward the laborer for throwing himself out of work, by giving him food better, and more abundant, than he obtained in independence. . . . They are governed by what they call their feelings, and those feelings are all on one side. Their pity for the pauper excludes any for the laborer, or for the rate-payer. They sympathize with idleness and improvidence, not with industry, frugality, and independence. . . . It is scarcely necessary to remind the reader of the well-known principle, that if relief be afforded on terms which do not render it less eligible than independent labor, the demand for it will increase, while there is a particle of property left to appease it."

However the Poor Law reform of 1834 may be considered by many today, it proved sufficiently satisfactory to successive British governments to be retained with only minor changes until the end of the nineteenth century. But there was mounting sentiment against it as the years wore on. Much of this was stirred up by the novels of Charles Dickens and others, with their lurid pictures of conditions in the workhouses. Toward the end of the century the more stringent regulations were gradually relaxed. In 1891 supplies of toys and books were permitted in the workhouses. In 1892 tobacco and snuff could be provided. In 1900 a government circular recommended the grant of outdoor relief [i.e., relief outside of the workhouses] for the aged of good character.

A new Royal Commission on the Poor Laws was set up in 1905. (One member was Beatrice Webb.) It brought in a report in 1909, but as the report was not unanimous, the Government took no action on it. However, new "social legislation" continued to be enacted. An Old Age Pensions Act was passed in 1908. And in 1909 David Lloyd George, the radical chancellor of the exchequer, anticipating President Lyndon Johnson's War on Poverty by more than half a century, exclaimed in introducing his new budget: "This is a war budget for raising money to wage implacable warfare against poverty and squalidness."

Finally, the National Insurance Act of 1911, providing sickness and unemployment benefits on a contributory basis to a selected group of industrial workers, marked the birth of the modern Welfare State, which reached maturity in England with the enactment of the Beveridge reforms in 1944.

But the Poor Law Commissioners of 1834, and the Parliament that enacted their recommendations, had frankly recognized and faced a problem that their political successors seem, as I have said, almost systematically to ignore—"the difficult problem," to quote once more the words in which Nassau Senior stated it, "how to afford to the poorer classes adequate relief without material injury to their diligence or their providence."

Is this problem soluble? Or does it present an inescapable dilemma? Can the State undertake to provide adequate relief to everybody who really needs and deserves it without finding itself supporting the idle, the improvident, and the swindlers? And can it frame rigid rules that would adequately protect it against fraud and imposture without as a result denying help to some of those really in need? Can the State, again, provide really "adequate" relief for any extended period even to the originally "deserving" without undermining or destroying their incentives to industry, frugality, and self-support? If people can get an "adequate" living without working, why work? Can the State, finally, provide "adequate" relief to all the unemployed, or, even more, guaranteed incomes for all, without undermining by excessive taxation the incentives of the working population that is forced to provide this support? Can the State, in sum, provide "adequate" relief to all without discouraging and gravely reducing the production out of which all relief must come?—without letting loose a runaway inflation?—without going bankrupt?

This apparent dilemma may be surmountable. But no relief system or welfare-state system so far embarked upon has satisfactorily surmounted it; and the problem certainly cannot be solved until the alternatives it presents are candidly recognized and examined.

CHAPTER 8

The Ballooning Welfare State

MOST OF THE SELF-STYLED LIBERALS OF THE PRESENT DAY WOULD BE astonished to learn that the father of the welfare state that they so much admire was none other than the fervent antiliberal and advocate of "blood and iron," Otto von Bismarck.

"He was the first statesman in Europe to devise a comprehensive scheme of social security, offering the worker insurance against accident, sickness, and old age. This Bismarckian 'socialism' later became a model for every other country in Europe. It represented in part the paternalistic function of the state which Bismarck, as a conservative, had always held."[1]

Bismarck's scheme of compulsory insurance went into effect in 1883, and was soon even baptized by German journalists *der Wohlfahrtsstaat.*

The example of Germany was followed by Austria in 1888 and by Hungary in 1891.

It was not until 1912 that compulsory health insurance was

1. "Bismarck," *Encyclopedia Britannica,* 1965.

introduced in Great Britain, under Lloyd George's National Insurance Act of 1911. In 1925 came contributory old-age, widows' and orphans' pensions. Unemployment insurance was put on a fresh basis in the Unemployment Act of 1934, which set up at the same time a national system of unemployment assistance. In 1945 the Family Allowance Act was passed. It provided for payment to every family, rich or poor, of an allowance for each child, other than the eldest. In 1946 came the National Health Service Act, offering free medical services and medicines to everyone.

Then, in 1948, as a result of the report of Sir William Beveridge, the whole system of compulsory contributions for social insurance was immensely extended, with wider unemployment benefits, sickness benefits, maternity benefits, widows' benefits, guardians' allowances, retirement pensions, and death grants.

The continuous expansion of "social security" and welfare services in Great Britain is typical of what has happened in most other countries in the Western world over the last half century. The broad pattern has been remarkably similar: a multitude of "insurance" programs, supported in part by compulsory contributions and in part by general tax funds, ostensibly protecting everyone against the hazards of poverty, unemployment, accident, sickness, old age, malnutrition, "substandard" housing, or almost any other imaginable lack; programs expanding year by year in the number of contingencies covered, in the number of beneficiaries under each program, in the size of individual benefits paid, and of course in the total financial burden imposed.

So year by year the tendency has been for every working person to pay a higher percentage of his earned income either for his own compulsory "insurance" or for the support of others. Year by year, also, the total burden of taxes tends to go up, both absolutely and proportionately. But direct and acknowledged taxes have tended to go up less than total expenditures.

This has led to chronic deficits that are met by printing more irredeemable paper money, and so to the almost universal chronic inflation that marks the present age.

Let us look at the ballooning welfare state in detail as it has developed in our own country.

We may begin with President Franklin D. Roosevelt's 1935 message to Congress in which he declared: "The Federal Government must and shall quit this business of relief. . . . Continued dependence upon relief induces a spiritual and moral disintegration, fundamentally destructive to the national fiber."

The contention was then made that if unemployment and old-age "insurance" were put into effect, poverty and distress would be relieved by contributory programs that did not destroy the incentives and self-respect of the recipients. Thus relief could gradually be tapered off to negligible levels.

The Social Security Act became law on August 4, 1935.

Let us see first of all what happened to the old-age provisions of that act. There have been constant additions and expansions of benefits. The act was overhauled as early as 1939. Coverage was broadened substantially in 1950. In 1952, 1954, 1956, 1958, and 1960 (note the correspondence with years of Congressional elections) there were further liberalizations of coverage or benefits. The 1965 amendments added Medicare for some 20 million beneficiaries. The 1967 amendments, among other liberalizations, increased payments to the 24 million beneficiaries by an average of 13 percent and raised minimum benefits 25 percent. In 1969 retirement and survivors benefits were raised again by about 15 percent, effective January 1, 1970.

(It is sometimes argued that these benefit increases from 1950 to 1970 were necessary to keep pace with increases in living costs. Actually the increases in individual monthly benefits totaled 83 percent, compared with a 51.3 percent increase in consumer prices over the same period.)

From 1937 to 1950, Social Security was financed by a combined tax rate of only 2 percent (1 percent each) on both employer and employee on wages up to $3,000 a year. Since then both the rates and the maximum wage base have been increased every few years. In 1972 the combined tax rate was 10.4 percent (5.2 percent on both employer and employee) on a maximum wage base that has been raised to $9,000. The result is that whereas the maximum annual payment up to 1950 was only $60, it had risen to $936.

On June 30, 1972 all previous benefit-increase records were broken. President Nixon had asked for an increase in Social Security benefits of 5 percent. The Republicans in Congress raised this to 10 percent. The Democrats insisted it should be 20 percent. And so 20 percent it was, by overwhelming majorities in both Houses. This came on the heels of two benefit hikes, enacted in 1970 and 1971, totaling 26.5 percent. In addition, Congress provided that effective in 1975 benefits would rise automatically to match every further rise of 3 percent or more in the consumer price index.

It was shrewdly provided that payment of the increased benefits would begin in checks mailed out in early October 1972 —just a month before the forthcoming Congressional and Presidential election. It was still more shrewdly provided that the increased payroll taxes to pay for the increased benefits would not start until the following January, long after the polls had closed. The combined tax rate was raised to 11 percent; but by providing for future increases in the wage-base rather than the flat tax rate itself, Congress threw most of the increased future tax burden on the higher-paid workers and their employers.

In 1947, payroll tax collections for old age and survivors' insurance amounted to $1.6 billion; by 1970, these taxes had increased to $39.7 billion. By fiscal 1973, total social insurance taxes and contributions were estimated at $63.7 billion.

At the beginning, the Social Security program was sold to the American public as a form of old-age "insurance." The taxes were represented as the "premiums" paid for this insurance. Everybody who was getting benefits was assured that he could accept these with no loss of "dignity," because he was "only getting what he had paid for."

This was never true, even at the beginning, and has become less true year by year. The low wage receivers have always been paid much more in proportion to their "premiums" than the higher wage receivers. The disparity has been increased with succeeding revisions of the act. The typical beneficiary even in 1968 was receiving benefits worth about five times the value of the payroll taxes he and his employer paid in.[2]

The OASDI program has developed into a mixed system of insurance and welfare handouts, with the welfare element getting constantly larger. It is today a bad system judged either as insurance or as welfare. On the one hand, benefits in excess of the amounts they paid for are being given, in some cases, to persons who are not in need of welfare. On the other hand, persons who are in fact receiving welfare handouts are being taught to believe that they are getting only "earned" insurance. Obviously, welfare programs can be expanded even faster than otherwise if they are masked as "contributory insurance" programs.

Our concern in the present chapter, however, is not with the defects of the OASDI program but primarily with its rate of growth. In 1947, social security benefit payments covered only old-age and survivors' insurance and amounted to less than half a billion. In 1956, disability insurance was added, and in 1965 health insurance. In 1972, these payments reached more than $39 billion.

2. Colin D. Campbell and Rosemary G. Campbell, "Cost-Benefit Ratios under the Federal Old-age Insurance Program," U.S. Joint Economic Committee, Old-age Income Assurance, Part III, Washington, D.C., U.S. Government Printing Office, December, 1967, pp. 72–84.

Unemployment Insurance

Now let us look at unemployment insurance. This program was also set up under the Social Security Act of 1935. But whereas old-age insurance was on a strictly national basis, unemployment insurance was instituted on a state-by-state basis within the broad scope of certain Federal criteria.

While provisions have differed in each of the fifty states, unemployment insurance has shown the same chronic growth tendency as old-age benefits. In 1937, the states typically required periods of two or three weeks before any benefits were paid. The theory behind this was that a man just out of employment would have at least some minimum savings; that the state would be given time to determine his benefit rights; and that the benefit funds should be conserved for more serious contingencies by reducing or eliminating payments for short periods of unemployment. Now the waiting period has been reduced to only one week, and in some states does not exist at all.

In contrast with the $15 to $18 weekly benefit ceilings in various states in 1940, the maximums now range between $40 and $86 a week, exclusive of dependents' allowances in some states.

Reflecting both legislated increases and rising wage levels, nationwide average weekly benefit payments increased from $10.56 in 1940 to $57.72 in 1971. Even after allowing for higher consumer prices, the real increase in purchasing power of these average benefits was 63 percent, and they continue to increase much faster than either wages or prices.

As of 1971, state legislation had increased the maximum duration of unemployment benefits from the predominantly prevailing 16-week level in 1940 to 26 weeks in 41 states—and of longer duration ranging to 39 weeks in the other states. In December, 1971, Congress voted to provide 13 weeks' additional benefits in states with sustained unemployment rates of more than 6½ percent. This made it possible for workers in such eligible areas to draw such benefits up to a total of 52 consecutive weeks.

Total annual benefit payments increased from about one half billion dollars in 1940 to $3.8 billion in 1970—more than a seven-fold increase, and the highest payout up to that time. In 1970 alone total benefits increased 80 percent ($1.7 billion) over the 1969 level. The combination of legislated increases in maximum weekly benefits and in maximum duration of the benefits has increased nearly *tenfold* the total benefits potentially payable to the individual unemployed worker in a year's period (dollars per week multiplied by the number of weeks).[3]

This is bound to increase still further. On July 8, 1969, President Nixon called upon the states to provide for higher weekly unemployment compensation benefits. He suggested that weekly maximums be set at two thirds of the average weekly wage in a state so that benefits of 50 percent of wages would be paid to at least 80 percent of insured workers. Outlays for unemployment insurance benefits were estimated for fiscal 1972 at $7.2 billion.

There can be no doubt that unemployment compensation reduces the incentive to hold on to an old job or to find a new one. It helps unions to maintain artificially high wage rates, and it prolongs and increases unemployment. One economist has likened it to "a bounty for keeping out of the labor market."[4].

This argument, of course, can be extended. Not merely unemployment compensation, but any form of relief, tends to take people off the labor market, and to reduce employment. When people are taken "adequate" care of by relief, and allowed to stay on that relief, they do not have to seek work. With their competition removed, wage-rates can be kept higher than oth-

3. Some of the foregoing material on Social Security and unemployment compensation is derived from studies by the American Enterprise Institute, Washington, D.C.
4. W. H. Hutt, *The Theory of Idle Resources*, London, Jonathan Cape, 1939, p. 129

erwise. But at these higher wage-rates, fewer jobs will be available. So though temporary unemployment seems to create the need for relief, the relief, once supplied and made "adequate" and long-term, tends to make the unemployment permanent—an ominous circle.

To return to unemployment compensation, it is a complete misnomer to call it unemployment "insurance." In the United States the workers do not even make a direct contribution to it (though in the long run it must tend to reduce the real pay of the steady worker). Like so-called government old-age "insurance," it is in fact a confused mixture of insurance and handout. Those who are continually urging an increase in the percentage of the previous wage rate paid, or the extension of the benefit-paying period (to avoid undisguised relief), forget that it violates ordinary welfare standards of equity by paying larger sums to the previously better paid workers than to the previously lower paid workers.

But apart from these shortcomings, what we are primarily concerned with here is the tendency of unemployment compensation, once adopted, to keep growing both as a percentage of weekly wages and in the length of idle time for which it is paid.

How little success the increasingly costly Social Security and unemployment compensation programs have had in enabling the Federal Government to "quit this business of relief" we shall see in the next chapter.

CHAPTER 9

Welfarism Gone Wild

BOTH SOCIAL SECURITY AND UNEMPLOYMENT COMPENSATION WERE proposed in large part on the argument of Franklin D. Roosevelt and others in 1935 that they would enable the government to "quit this business of relief."

Though all the social "insurance" programs he asked for were enacted, together with a score of others, and though all of these supplementary or "substitute" programs have been constantly enlarged, direct relief, instead of showing any tendency to diminish, has increased beyond anything dreamed of in 1935.

The number of welfare recipients in New York City alone jumped from 328,000 in 1960 to 1,275,000 in August, 1972 (exceeding the total population of Baltimore) and was still growing. On March 10, 1971, the U.S. Department of Health, Education and Welfare reported that more than 10 percent of the residents of the nation's twenty largest cities were on welfare. In New York City, Baltimore, St. Louis, and San Francisco, it was one person in seven; and in Boston, one in five. The Mayor of Newark, N.J., told Congress on January 22, 1971, that 30 percent of the population in his city was on relief.

For the whole country, the number of people on welfare grew from 6,052,000 in 1950 to 7,098,000 in 1960, to 9,540,000 in 1968, to 14,407,000 in April, 1971, and to 15,069,000 in April, 1972.

Because payments to individuals kept increasing, total expenditures for relief grew still faster. Here is a condensed record:

Fiscal Year	All Funds (000)	Federal Funds (000)
1936	$ 349,892	$ 20,202
1940	1,123,660	279,404
1945	1,028,000	417,570
1950	2,488,831	1,095,788
1955	2,939,570	1,440,771
1960	4,039,433	2,055,226
1965	5,868,357	3,178,850
1970	14,433,500	7,594,300
1971	18,631,600	9,932,000

Sources: U.S. Department of Health, Education and Welfare, NCSS Report F-5, July 6, 1971; and *Social Security Bulletin*, December, 1971.

In the fiscal year 1971, relief expenditures at $18.6 billion were running at more than four times the rate of 1960, more than sixteen times the rate of 1940, and more than 53 times the rate of 1936.

To economize on figures, I have not only confined myself to five-year interval comparisons, but I have not shown the division between state and local funds. Yet these comparisons are part of the explanation of the skyrocketing growth of these relief figures. It will be noticed that while the Federal contribution to direct relief expenditures was only 5 percent in 1936, it was 25 percent in 1940, 44 percent in 1950, and 53 percent in 1971. Yet relief was actually administered at the state and local level. In fact, it was for the most part administered by the cities and counties. The localities contributed only 26 percent toward the total cost of the relief they handed out in 1940, only 11 percent in 1950, 13 percent in 1960, and 11 percent in 1970. When a city government is contributing only 11 cents of its own for every dollar it pays out to relief recipients, it can distribute its political favors cheaply, and has little incentive to exercise vigilance against overpayment and fraud.

Most of those who discuss the mounting cost of direct relief treat this figure in isolation as if it represented the total cost of "the war against poverty." In fact, it is only a small fraction of that cost, recently running in the neighborhood of not much more than a tenth. The following figures are from an official table of "Social Welfare Expenditures Under Public Programs."[1]

SOCIAL WELFARE EXPENDITURES
(in millions of dollars)

Year	Total	Federal	State and Local
1935	$ 6,548	$ 3,207	$ 3,341
1940	8,795	3,443	5,351
1945	9,205	4,399	4,866
1950	23,508	10,541	12,967
1955	32,640	14,623	18,017
1960	52,293	24,957	27,337
1965	77,121	37,720	39,401
1968	113,839	60,314	53,525
1970	145,350	77,321	68,029
1971 (p.)	170,752	92,411	78,341

This gigantic total of $171 billion for "social welfare" is more than triple the figure for 1960 and more than 26 times the figure for 1935. Yet the 29-fold increase in Federal expenditures for welfare in the 36-year period, instead of reducing the burden on the states and cities, as originally promised, has been ac-

1. Statistical Abstract of the United States: 1971, Table 430, p. 271, and *Social Security Bulletin,* December, 1971.

companied by a 23-fold increase even in that local burden.

A similar result is evident if we consider the cost of direct relief alone. Though the Federal Government was contributing only 5 percent of that total cost in 1936 compared with 53 percent in 1971, the cost to the states and localities has increased 26-fold. So much for the theory that "revenue-sharing," or increased Federal contributions, do anything in the long run to reduce the burden of welfare spending on the states and localities. They lead merely to a total increase in that spending.

So the tendency of welfare spending in the United States has been to increase at an exponential rate. This has also been its tendency elsewhere. Only when the economic and budgetary consequences of this escalation become so grave that they are obvious to the majority of the people—i.e., only when irreparable damage has been done—are the welfare programs likely to be curbed. The chronic inflation of the last 25 to 35 years in nearly every country in the world has been mainly the consequence of welfarism run wild.

The causes of this accelerative increase are hardly mysterious. Once the premise has been accepted that "the poor," as such, have a "right" to share in somebody else's income—regardless of the reasons why they are poor or others are better off—there is no logical stopping place in distributing money and favors to them, short of the point where this brings about equality of income for all. If I have a "right" to a "minimum income sufficient to live in decency," whether I am willing to work for it or not, why don't I also have a "right" to just as much income as you have, regardless of whether you earn it and I don't?

Once the premise is accepted that poverty is never the fault of the poor but the fault of "society" (i.e., of the self-supporting), or of "the capitalist system," then there is no definable limit to be set on relief, and the politicians who want to be elected or reelected will compete with each other in proposing new "welfare" programs to fill some hitherto "unmet need," or in propos-

ing to increase the benefits or reduce the eligibility requirements of some existing program.

Uncounted Programs

No complete count seems to exist anywhere of the present
total number of welfare programs. The $171 billion expendi-
ture for social welfare in the fiscal year 1971 is officially divided
into roughly $66 billion for "social insurance," $22 billion for
"public aid," $11 billion for "health and medical programs,"
$10 billion for "veterans' programs," $56 billion for "education," nearly $1 billion for "housing," and $5 billion for "other
social welfare." But these subtotals are in turn made up of 47
different groups of programs, and many of these in turn consist
of many separate programs.[2]

The bewildered taxpayer reads about such things as food
stamps, job training, public housing, rent supplements, "model
cities," community-action projects, legal services for the poor,
neighborhood health centers, FAP, Office of Economic Opportunity (OEO), Medicaid, Old Age Assistance (OAA), Aid to the
Blind (AB), Aid to the Permanently and Totally Disabled
(APTD), Aid to Families with Dependent Children (AFDC),
General Assistance (GA), Community Action Program (CAP),
the Job Corps, manpower training programs, Head Start,
VISTA, and on and on, and has no idea whether one is included
under another, whether they duplicate each other's functions,
which, if any, have been discontinued, or which are just about
to start. All he knows is that there seems to be a new one every
month.

In 1969, Mrs. Edith Green, a Democratic Congresswoman
from Oregon, asked the Library of Congress to compile the total
amount of funds a family could receive from the Federal Government if that family took advantage of all the public assistance programs that were available.

2. See *Social Security Bulletin,* December, 1971.

Taking a hypothetical family of a mother with four children —one a preschooler, one in elementary school, one in high school and one in college—the library informed her of the following:

This family could collect $2,800 from public assistance; $618 from medical assistance because of AFDC; $336 in cash value for food stamps; and about $200 from OEO for legal services and health care. The family would also be entitled to public housing or rent supplements ranging in value from $406 to $636.

The preschool child would be entitled to enter Head Start, the average cost being $1,050 for each youngster. The child in high school would be eligible for $1,440 worth of services from Upward Bound and the youngster in college would be eligible for an education opportunity grant that could be worth anywhere from $500 to $1,000. He also would be eligible for a National Defense Education Act loan, and if he took advantage of the forgiveness feature, he could get an outright grant of $520. He would also be eligible for a work-study program costing in the neighborhood of $475. If the mother wanted to participate in the job opportunity program, this would be worth $3,000.

So this imaginary family, a mother with four children, would be able to take advantage of grants and services worth $11,513 for the year.

In another hypothetical case, a mother with eight children could total an annual welfare income of $21,093.[3]

In 1968, Congressman William V. Roth, Jr., and his staff were able to identify 1,571 programs, including 478 in the Department of Health, Education and Welfare alone, but concluded that "no one, anywhere, knows exactly how many Federal programs there are."

In February, 1972, Administration witnesses testified before a Congressional committee that there were 168 separate Fed-

3. *Human Events,* December 13, 1969.

98

eral programs geared in whole or in part to combating poverty.[4] But as the total expenditures of these 168 programs were only $31.5 billion (out of $92 billion of Federal "social welfare expenditures") this must have been an incomplete list.

While the Federal Government keeps piling up new welfare programs, under Democratic or Republican Administrations, almost every individual program shows a tendency to snowball. One reason is that when Congressmen propose a new program, the expenditure set in the initial year is almost always comparatively moderate, to allay opposition—the "entering wedge" technique; but annual increases in spending are built into the law. Another reason is that when a new welfare program is launched, it takes people a little while to catch on to it; and then the stampede begins. A still further reason is that the bureaucrats who administer the program—eager to demonstrate their own vicarious compassion and liberality, as well as the indispensability of their jobs—not only interpret the eligibility requirements very leniently, but actively campaign to advise potential "clients" of their "legal right" to get on the rolls.

In short, one reason that the relief rolls soared in the 1960's was that there was a substantial body of people employed by the Federal government itself to see that they soared. As Nathan Glazer spelled it out: "There were 100,000 workers in Community Action Agencies, established under the Office of Economic Opportunity after 1964. One of the major tasks of this legion was to tell poor people about welfare, accompany them to welfare agencies, argue for them, organize them in sit-ins, distribute simplified accounts of the rules governing welfare and the benefits available. In short, there were 100,000 recruiters for welfare that were not there before. In addition, there were at least 1,800 lawyers paid for by OEO projects in 1968; one of their functions was to challenge the restrictions around the

4. *New York Times,* February 16, 1972.

granting of welfare. . . . Litigation eliminated restrictive practices and intimidated welfare agencies and workers into accepting more on the rolls and into giving them more."[5]

How Many Cheat?

There has been a great deal of discussion in the last few years regarding the extent of fraud and cheating among those on relief. From the very nature of the problem this can never be exactly known; but the evidence indicates that it is substantial.

In January, 1971, after a door-to-door check on welfare cases, the State of Nevada struck about 22 percent of the recipients—3,000 people—from the relief rolls. The State Welfare Director reported that they had been cheating taxpayers out of a million dollars a year through failure to report income from other sources, including unemployment benefits. The director blamed the frauds on a Federal regulation that permitted welfare applicants to obtain aid simply by stating that they met all qualifications.

In Michigan, state welfare officials discovered cases of money being pocketed by welfare clients for dental work which was never performed.

In California, a group of San Francisco Bay area residents—all fully employed—conducted an experiment to prove to county supervisors how easy it is to get on relief. They traveled the circuit of welfare offices, applying for and getting on welfare, usually without even furnishing identification. Governor Reagan said that "one managed to get on welfare four times under four different names in one day—all at the same office."

In his message to the California legislature, Governor Reagan pointed out: "The same government that requires a taxpaying citizen to document every statement on his tax return decrees that questioning a welfare applicant demeans and humiliates him."

5. *New York* magazine, October 11, 1971.

A spot check of welfare rolls in New York City by the General Accounting Office, reported in September, 1969, showed that 10.7 percent of all families on relief there did not meet the eligibility requirements, and that 34.1 percent of those who were eligible were being overpaid.[6]

In 1971, New York City Comptroller Abraham Beame revealed that the city was losing $2 million a year as a result of forged checks. More millions were lost because people on relief falsely complained that they had not received their checks; they were mailed duplicates. Simply requiring those on relief to come and pick up their checks, rather than getting them by mail, lowered New York City's welfare lists by about 20 percent.

It is impossible to know how much of the blame for the national and local welfare mess is to be put on relief cheaters and how much on loose administration. It is made so easy to get and stay on relief legally that cheating has become less and less necessary.

On January 12, 1969, *The New York Times* ran a front-page story under the headline: "Millions in City Poverty Funds Lost by Fraud and Inefficiency." It reported that "Multiple investigations of the city's $122-million-a-year antipoverty program are disclosing chronic corruption and administrative chaos," and quoted an assistant district attorney as saying: "It's so bad that it will take ten years to find out what's really been going on inside the Human Resources Administration." The next day Secretary of Labor W. Willard Wirtz said that New York City had the worst administrative problems of any antipoverty program in any city in the country.

But the New York situation kept getting worse. In January, 1971, a welfare mother and her four children were assigned to the Waldorf Astoria, one of New York's most elegant hotels, at

6. These examples were cited in an article "Welfare Out of Control" in *U. S. News & World Report,* February 8, 1971. By coincidence, *Time* and *Newsweek* also carried long feature stories on welfare in their issues of the same date, covering similar material.

a cost of $152.64 for two days. The city's welfare agency claimed with a straight face that there was no room elsewhere. But many other routine practices of the city were almost as costly, with entire hotels "temporarily" filled with relief families at hotel rates. One family was put up at the Broadway Central at a cost of $390.50 a week. Another, a welfare family of fifteen, was put up at a Bronx motel at a rental that would add up to $54,080 a year.[7]

Much the fastest growing relief program has been Aid to Families with Dependent Children (AFDC). In the ten years from 1960 to 1970 the number of people aided by this program increased from 3,023,000 to 9,500,000. Costs soared from $621 million in 1955 to $4.1 billion in 1970. Recipients had reached 10,933,000 in April, 1972, and costs were running at an annual rate of $7 billion.

The nationwide cheating on this is probably higher than on any other welfare program. The reason is that a mother and her children, legitimate or illegitimate, become eligible for AFDC relief if there is no employed father present. The mothers report that the father has "deserted." "The fact is," according to one authority, "that in many cases the father never really deserts. He just stays out of sight so the woman can get on AFDC rolls. In slum areas, everyone knows this goes on. It is widespread in New York City." Governor Reagan reported that he knew there were 250,000 homes in California where the father had run out.

There is another factor. In Essex County, New Jersey, a survey of 750 mothers on Aid-for-Dependent-Children relief found 49 percent of the mothers to be "single girls with out-of-wedlock children."[8] Having illegitimate children was an automatic way of getting on relief.

California's state director of social welfare, Robert Carleson, revealed in October, 1972, that a special computerized check of

7. *Time,* February 8, 1971.
8. *New York Times,* April 23, 1972.

102

welfare receipient earnings disclosed a 41 percent rate of apparent fraud in the "Aid to Families with Dependent Children" program.

One of the fundamental causes for the huge and growing load of relief cases is that there is no adequate investigation of eligibility. The excuse offered by some welfare workers is: "It's impossible to do adequate eligibility checks. There isn't time. It's a question of helping people who need help rather than catching people who need catching."

One result of this attitude was illustrated in March, 1972, when the New York State Inspector General turned up, among others, the case of a twenty-two-year-old Brooklyn man who had managed to get welfare aid from six different Brooklyn centers, while also receiving welfare under his mother's Aid to Dependent Children case, payments that should have ended when he turned 18.[9]

Still another reason why there is no adequate investigation of eligibility is that Federal bureaucratic regulations discourage it. As Governor Reagan has put it: "The regulations are interpreted to mean that no caseworker can challenge or question a welfare applicant's statements."[10]

Instead of trying to reform this situation, the Department of Health, Education and Welfare seems mainly concerned to defend it. It has published and circulated widely a booklet called *Welfare Myths vs. Facts.* This turns legitimate criticisms into "myths" by grossly overstating them, and then produces questionable answers. For example:

"Myth: The welfare rolls are full of able-bodied loafers.

"Fact: Less than 1% of welfare recipients are able-bodied unemployed males."

This figure, implying that it would have a negligible effect on welfare to find jobs for these men, is incredibly low. It is apparently achieved by treating any physical impairment, however

9. *New York Times,* April 2, 1972.
10. *U.S. News & World Report,* March 1, 1971.

trivial, as a qualification for family relief; it ignores employable women; and it ignores the fact that the average relief family consists of 3.7 persons, who would move off the rolls if the breadwinner went to work. Another example:

"Myth: Once on welfare, always on welfare.

"Fact: The average welfare family has been on the rolls for 23 months. . . . The number of long-term cases is relatively small."

A 23-month *average* for families on relief is hardly something to be complacent about, even if the figure is accurate. The department's own charts show that more than a third of those on welfare have been there three years or more. Moreover, the department's average does not count "repeaters." If a family were on relief for, say, 23 months, off a month, back on for another 23 months, and so on, it would not raise the average. Nor does any figure based on relief at any given point in time count the prospective remaining period each case will be on the rolls. Already families have been found on relief for three generations.[11]

Small wonder that President Nixon, in his State of the Union message of January, 1971, called the existing American relief system "a monstrous, consuming outrage."

11. An excellent analysis of the HEW *Welfare Myths vs. Facts* pamphlet appeared in *The Wall Street Journal* of January 27, 1972, by Richard A. Snyder, a member of the Pennyslvania senate.

CHAPTER 10

The Fallacy of "Providing Jobs"

Since ancient times it has been assumed not only that the government has a duty to do something for the poor, but that one of the things it can and should do is to "provide jobs." A declared objective, in fact, even of the Elizabethan Poor Law was the "setting of the poor to work." Today many are insisting that the government has both the ability and the duty to become "the employer of last resort," or to "guarantee everybody a job."

These views rest on some serious misconceptions.

In a hypothetical evenly rotating economy, with free and fluid competition, each worker would try to find work wherever his pay was highest, which means wherever his marginal productivity was highest; and each employer would likewise try to find the worker whose productivity was highest for the pay and in the job he had to offer. Therefore in such an economy workers would be allocated at their highest individual productivity among the tens of thousands of different occupations, and there would tend to be full employment at maximum overall productivity. There would be no unemployment for the State to try to eliminate.

In any actual dynamic economy, of course, there is always a certain amount of "normal" unemployment. This is too often regarded as an unmitigated evil. It is misleadingly called "frictional" unemployment. Yet it is mainly the result of necessary and desirable economic adjustments that ordinarily take time, and for the most part ought to be allowed to take time.

In a healthy, flexible economy these adjustments are always taking place. Some industries are expanding while others are shrinking, either absolutely or comparatively. It is necessary that workers and capital transfer from the shrinking to the expanding industries. Some workers are forced to do this because they are laid off. Others quit voluntarily, draw unemployment benefits, live on their savings, give themselves vacations, rest between jobs, or spend time "looking around" and deciding what to do next. They are trying to decide where they can be most profitably or satisfactorily employed; and time for comparisons is necessary to ensure a good choice.

A man is only unemployed, as the economist A. C. Pigou once put it, "when he is *both* not employed and *also* desires to be employed." It is this subjective element that statisticians cannot measure. So both those who are voluntarily and those who are involuntarily between jobs are lumped together in the same unemployment statistics.

Many people are unduly distressed by these statistics not only because they fail to make this distinction but because they picture the unemployed as a permanent army hopelessly tramping around in search of work. But the make-up of the unemployed is constantly changing. In mid-1972, to take a fairly typical example, the average duration of unemployment was eleven weeks. Only about a fifth of the unemployed were out of work for fifteen weeks or more.

It is when there is abnormal or mass unemployment that the

demand is loudest that the government itself should provide jobs. What is first of all wrong with this demand is that it ignores the cause of the existing unemployment. In most cases this cause will be found to be some policy or situation for which the government itself is mainly responsible.

If the government has imposed a minimum wage law, for example, it has in effect condemned to unemployment all the workers incapable of earning that minimum. If, then, the government itself "provides work" for them, it is at best doing merely what it has prevented private employers from doing. If it pays these workers the legal minimum, as it probably would, it is employing them at an economic loss made up by the taxpayers, for such workers are almost certainly producing less value than the amount of their pay.

Private employers would at least have employed them (if there had been no minimum wage law) where their productive value was highest. As the government will be under no such necessity, it will not try to do this. So on the average it will put them to even less productive work than private industry would have done.

If, again, the government tries to put the unemployed to work in lines in which there are already strong unions, it will run into opposition from these unions for increasing the competition against their members. This will further restrict the productive possibilities of whatever work the government offers.

The same kind of problems will arise no matter what the primary cause of the existing unemployment. That cause may be, as it often is, excessive wage rates brought about by labor union pressure—by strikes or strike threats, or by concessions otherwise wrung from employers because of legal compulsions imposed on them to "bargain collectively" with specified unions. Excessive wage rates always lead to unemployment. When the unemployed compete for private jobs, this tends, in a free market, to bring average wage rates back to levels at which unemployment will disappear. But if all those who are thrown out of work by excessive wage rates are then immediately employed by the government, the normal economic pressures are removed to get wages down to a working market level. The necessary adjustments are not made. The workers employed by the government are employed at a loss borne by the taxpayers. The whole economic community, because its workers are less efficiently employed, is made poorer than it otherwise would have been.

The same reasoning applies if the cause of the unemployment is a typical depression, brought about, for example, because a currency or credit deflation has led to a drop in consumer demand and commodity prices while wage rates and other "sticky" costs stay up. In a free market, this situation would eventually be cured by a downward adjustment of wage rates to the new lower demand level and price level. But if the government immediately offers make-work "jobs" to everybody dropped from employment by private industry, the downward adjustment of wage rates will never take place. The burden on the taxpayers will soon become unbearable; and the only way out will seem to be budget deficits and an inflation of the currency. Further inflation, in fact, will soon be considered the "normal" solution for all unemployment problems—until this has led to the inevitable crisis.

Step One: Re-examine Existing Policies

The first step necessary, therefore, when there is an abnormal amount of unemployment, is for the government in power to re-examine existing economic policies and discontinue all those that have been causing the unemployment.

A certain percentage of the unemployed are unemployables. These include the physically incapacitated—the aged, weak, disabled, or blind. They include the feeble-minded, and the people so backward that they cannot be taught elementary skills, and require more supervision than it is practicable to provide. They include, finally, the chronic loafers—the Rip van Winkles born with "an insuperable aversion to all kinds of profitable labor"—and the hostile, who refuse to accept any kind of discipline, who through malice or indifference do more damage than useful work. It is frustrating for any government to try to "provide useful work" for such people.

In times of mass unemployment there is nearly always a loud demand that the government should provide jobs rather than merely put people on relief, but the effort, if undertaken, soon begins to prove prohibitively expensive. In the depression of the 1930s, for instance, the Roosevelt regime set up the Works Progress Administration (WPA) to provide jobs. But as the workers needed raw materials, tools, machinery, and equipment, this employment proved extremely expensive per job provided. When this was discovered, the officials in charge tried to think of projects—and were praised for thinking of projects—that provided the maximum number of jobs per dollar expended; in other words, jobs requiring the least raw materials, machinery, and equipment. But what was overlooked was that such jobs—requiring the maximum hand labor in relation to capital equipment—were precisely the least efficient and least productive jobs that could have been thought of. (It is estimated that private industry today in the United States has invested about $30,000 per production worker.)

All this points to the folly of the proposal that the government can or should "guarantee everybody a job." With the fear of dismissal completely removed, such a guarantee would demoralize even workers who might be passably industrious and efficient in unguaranteed jobs. They would have no obligation to please the boss or anybody else. Suppose they started to arrive one or two hours late? Or quit two hours early? Or chronically reported sick? Or failed to show up at all except to collect their pay? Or broke more dishes than they washed—botched every job they were assigned to? Or refused to accept orders or any direction? Or stole? Or committed deliberate vandalism? Or beat up the boss? Their jobs would be guaranteed, wouldn't they?

Putting aside all questions of worker morale, how would the government decide where and on what to put people to work, and how many on this job and how many on that? Could it put everybody to work on his previous skill, if any, regardless of whether there was still any demand for the product of his services? Could it put men to producing goods for which there was no market?

And what pay scale would it offer? Would it pay high enough wages to prevent workers from being attracted back to private industry? Or even high enough to attract workers already employed in private industry? Would it, on the other hand, pay lower than the minimum in private industry? Would such low wages prove politically tenable?

We are forced to the conclusion that it is impossible for the government to provide useful and profitable work (apart from necessary governmental services themselves) outside of what is or would be provided by an unhampered private enterprise.

We come now to a contrasting proposal—that the government should deny relief to anybody who refuses to take a job offered to him. This is a proposal that has been constantly put forward in the history of relief but has as constantly run into difficulties. The first objection commonly raised is that the specific job offered may not be "suitable." The man to whom it is offered may complain that the wage offered is too low, or the job too disagreeable, or too "menial," or beneath his skill, or even beyond his strength. There will always be those who will denounce the work requirement as a form of "involuntary servitude."

Such a work requirement is often written into relief laws, but the officials in charge of relief usually lack the courage to enforce it. They are afraid of being accused of "letting people starve," so the requirement quickly becomes merely perfunctory.

Practically all forced work is economically unprofitable. Toward the end of the eighteenth century, in fact, parish authorities in England were reduced to such expedients as making men stand in the parish pound for so many hours, or obliging them to attend a roll call several times a day, or making them dig holes and fill them up again.

But there was one work requirement that did have a plausible basis. It was the keystone, in fact, of the Poor Law reform of 1834. This was that no able-bodied person would be given relief unless he was willing to live in a workhouse and perform the usually monotonous and uninteresting labor there assigned to him. The Commissioners who proposed that requirement did not assume that the work so performed would be economically very useful. On the other hand, it was not imposed as a mere punishment. It was imposed primarily as a *test,* a test that hopefully would separate the pretenders from those in dire need. If a man was really in danger of starving, it was argued, he would accept the workhouse; if he refused it, his condition could not be too bad.

In England this system lasted, with general public acquiescence, for some three quarters of a century. Yet even in the Victorian Age protests against it became increasingly insistent. It is doubtful that it will ever again gain public acceptance.

We seem driven, then, to the conclusion that the government can neither guarantee useful and profitable work, nor directly provide it, nor compel it.

Is there any escape from this conclusion? Can the State devise—and have the courage consistently to adhere to—some work test, or work-acceptance test, that will enable it to separate the deserving poor from the shirkers and fakers? There is no more stubborn social problem than this: How can the State adequately relieve those truly in need without undermining their incentives to effort and without imposing on workers and producers an insupportable burden of relief?

This is a problem that no nation has yet satisfactorily solved.

But we have learned this: The chief thing that the State can do to reduce the problems of poverty and unemployment to minor dimensions is to permit and encourage the free market system to function.

CHAPTER 11

Should We Divide the Wealth?

FROM TIME IMMEMORIAL THERE HAVE BEEN REFORMERS WHO DE-
manded that wealth and income should be "divided equally"—
or at least divided with less glaring inequalities than the reformers saw around them.

These demands have never been more insistent than they are
today. Yet most of them are based, in the first place, on a completely erroneous idea of the extent to which present wealth or
income in the United States is "maldistributed." An American
socialist, Daniel De Leon, announced in a celebrated speech in
1905 that, on the average, the owners of American industry
grabbed off 80 percent of the wealth produced in their factories,
while the workers got only 20 percent.[1] His contention was
widely accepted and exerted great influence.

Yet the truth, as we have seen in the chapter on "The Distribution of Income," is exactly the opposite. Labor in America is

1. See Howard E. Kershner, *Dividing the Wealth*, Devin-Adair, 1971, pp.
17–24.

getting the lion's share of the nation's output. In recent years the employees of the country's corporations have been getting more than seven-eighths of the corporate income available for division, and the shareowners less than an eighth. More than 70 percent of the nation's personal income in 1970 was received in the form of wages and salaries. Business and professional income totaled less than 7 percent, interest payments only 8 percent, and dividends only 3 percent.

The truth seems to be that personal income in this country is already distributed roughly in proportion to each person's current contribution to output as measured in its market value. Some people, of course, inherit more wealth than others, and this affects their total personal income. How large a role this plays is statistically difficult to determine, but the income distribution figures just cited would indicate that the role is minor. As a percentage of the total population, there are today very few "idle rich," however conspicuous a few playboys may make themselves at the night clubs and gaudy playgrounds of the world.

Moreover, the "surplus" money simply doesn't exist to raise mass incomes very much. American tourists, visiting some backward country, may see poverty more widespread and abject than any they had ever imagined, and then notice also a few people driving around in Cadillacs, and here and there an ostentatious mansion; and they are often tempted to think that if only the wealth of these rich could be divided among these poor, at least half the economic problems of that country would be solved. What such casual travellers persistently forget is that these very rich may constitute only one person in a hundred or even one in a thousand, and that an equal distribution of their entire wealth among everyone would (provided the forced distribution itself did not prove economically demoralizing) raise average wealth by only an insignificant amount.

Suppose we take our own affluent country. In 1968, only one in every 900 returns reported an annual income of $100,000 or more. Out of a total of 61 million taxpayers, 383,000, or six tenths of 1 percent, paid taxes on incomes of $50,000 or more. Their total adjusted gross income came to some $37 billion, or 6.6 percent of total gross incomes reported. Out of this amount they paid a little more than $13 billion, or 36 percent of their income, in taxes. This left them with about $24 billion for themselves.

Suppose the government had seized the whole of this and distributed it among the 200 million total population. This would have come to $120 per person. As the disposable personal per capita income in 1968 was $2,939, this expropriation would have raised the average income of the recipients by only 4 percent to $3,059. (Per capita income actually rose anyway to $3,108 in 1969 and to $3,333 in 1970.) Of course if the government resorted to any such violent expropriation, it could not repeat it after the first year, for the simple reason that people would cease earning incomes of $50,000 a year or more to be seized.

Any attempt to equalize wealth and income by forced redistribution must destroy wealth and income. We can recognize this most clearly if we begin with the extreme case. If the median income per family has been $10,000 a year, and we decide that every family must be guaranteed exactly that and no family can be allowed to retain more than that, then we will destroy all economic incentives to work, earn, improve one's skills, or save. Those who had been getting less than that would no longer need to work for it; those who had been getting more would no longer see the point in working for the surplus to be seized, or even in working at all, since their income would be "guaranteed" in any case. People could be got to work only by coercion; most labor would be forced labor, and very little of it would be skilled or efficient.

The so-called "instinct of workmanship," without economic rewards, would have nothing to guide it into one channel rather than another, and nothing to hold it beyond the point of fatigue. Useful and profitable work would be black-market work. Those who survived would do so at a near-subsistence level.

A Guaranteed Annual Income

But the same kind of results, less extreme in degree, would follow from less extreme redistribution measures. The most fashionable of these at the moment is the Guaranteed Annual Income. I have already analyzed this at length, together with its most popular variant, the Negative Income Tax, in my book *Man vs. the Welfare State,*[2] and will only briefly indicate the objections to it here.

A guaranteed minimum income would not have quite the universal destructive effect on incentives as would an attempt to impose a compulsorily equal income, with the ceiling made identical with the floor. At least people earning incomes above the minimum guarantee, though they would be oppressively taxed, would still have some incentive to continue earning whatever surplus they were allowed to retain. But all those guaranteed a minimum income, whether they worked or not, would have no incentive to work at all if the guaranteed minimum were above what they had previously been earning for their work; and they would have very little incentive to work even if they had previously been earning, or were capable of earning, only a moderate amount above the guarantee.

It is clearly wrong in principle to allow the government forcibly to seize money from the people who work and to give it unconditionally to other able-bodied people whether they accept work or not. It is wrong in principle to give money to people solely because they say they haven't any—and especially to support such people on a permanent and not merely on a temporary emergency basis. It is wrong in principle to force

2. Henry Hazlitt, *Man vs. the Welfare State,* New Rochelle, N. Y.: Arlington House, 1969, pp. 62–100.

Welfare aid in 59 categories

Welfare is often thought of as food stamps and cash payments. But according to the Domestic Policy Council, in its report to President Reagan, there are 59 major public-assistance programs in America. They are:

■ CASH PROGRAMS

Aid to Families with Dependent Children
Supplemenal Social Security Income
Pensions for Wartime Veterans
Earned Income Tax Credit
Foster Care
Refugee Ressettlement Program
Emergency Assistance to Needy Families
Veterans Parents Compensation
Adoption Assistance
Indian General Assistance

FOOD PROGRAMS

Food Stamps
National School Lunch Program
Special Supplemental Feeding Program for Women, Infants, and Children
Temporary Emergency Assistance Program
Nutrition Assistance Program for Puerto Rico
Child Care Food Program
School Breakfast Program
Food Donations to Charitable Institutions
Summer Food Service Program for Children
Commodity Supplemental Food Program
Needy Family Program
Special Milk Program

HOUSING PROGRAMS

Housing Assistance Payments (Section 8 and rent supplements)
Public and Indian Housing
Low Income Home Energy Assistance Program
Interest Reduction Program
Homeownership Assistance Program
Weatherization Assistance

Rural Rental Assistance Program
Emergency Food and Shelter Program
Indian Housing Improvement Program

HEALTH PROGRAMS

Medicaid
Veterans Health Care
Maternal and Child Health Services Block Grant
Indian Health Service
Community Health Centers
Migrant Health Centers

SERVICE PROGRAMS

Social Services Block Grant
Head Start
Community Services Block Grant
Legal Aid
Family Planning Services

EMPLOYMENT PROGRAMS

Training Services for the Disadvantaged
Summer Youth Employment Program
Job Corps
Senior Community Service Employment Program
Work Incentive Program and Demonstrations
Native American Employment and Training Program
Seasonal Farmworkers Program
Foster Grandparent Program
Senior Companion Program

EDUCATION PROGRAMS

Pell Grants
Grants to local education agencies: Educationally Deprived Children
College Work-Study
Supplemental Education Opportunity Grants
State Student Incentive Grants
Upward Bound
Special Services for Disadvantaged Students
Talent Search

Cure-all

Welfare in Ohio

...y 1986, 43 per-
...amilies in Ohio
...ks from

have more children. A family of three receives $309 a month, or $103 per person. A family of...

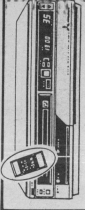

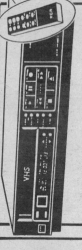

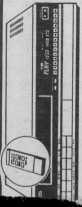

the workers and earners indefinitely to support the nonworkers and nonearners.

This must undermine the incentives of both the workers and the nonworkers. It puts a premium on idleness. It is an elementary requirement of economic incentive as well as justice that the man who works for a living should always be better off because of that, other things being equal, than the man who refuses to work for a living.

We have to face the fact that there are a substantial number of people who would rather live in near-destitution without working than to live comfortably at the cost of accepting the disciplines of a steady job. The higher we raise the income guarantee (and once we adopted it, the political pressures would be for raising it constantly), the greater the number of people who would see no reason to work.

A "Negative Income Tax"

Nor would a so-called "Negative Income Tax" do much to solve the problem. The Negative Income Tax is merely a misleading euphemism for a tapered-off guaranteed minimum income. The proposal is that for every dollar that a man earns for himself, his government income subsidy would be reduced, say, only 50 cents, instead of being reduced by the whole amount that he earns. In this way, it is argued, his incentive for self-support would not be entirely destroyed; for every dollar he earned for himself he would be able to retain at least half.

This proposal has a certain surface plausibility. Some prominent economists espouse it. In fact, the present writer put it forward himself more than thirty years ago,[3] but abandoned it shortly thereafter when its flaws became evident to him. Let us look at some of these:

1. The NIT (negative income tax), by neglecting the careful applicant-by-applicant investigation of needs and resources

3. In *The Annalist* (published by *The New York Times*), January 4, 1939.

made by the traditional relief system, would, like a flat guaranteed income, open the government to massive fraud. It would also, like the flat guaranteed income, force the government to support a family whether or not it was making any effort to support itself.

2. It is true that the NIT would not destroy incentives quite as completely as the flat guaranteed income, but it would seriously undermine them nonetheless. It would still give millions of people a guaranteed income whether they worked or not. Once more we must keep in mind that there are a substantial number of people who prefer near-destitution in idleness to a comfortable living at the cost of working. It is true that under the NIT scheme they would be allowed to keep half of anything they earned for themselves up to nearly twice the amount of the basic NIT benefit, but they would tend to look upon this as the equivalent of a tax of 50 percent on these earnings, and many would not think such earnings worth the trouble.

3. The NIT might prove even more expensive for the taxpayers than the flat guaranteed income. The sponsors of NIT, in their original monetary illustrations, proposed that the "break-off point" of their scheme would be something like the official "poverty-threshold" income—which is now (1972) about $4,320 for a nonfarm family of four. At this point no NIT benefits would be paid. If the family's income was only $3,320, falling short of the poverty-line income by $1,000, than a $500 NIT benefit would be paid. And if the family's earned income was zero, then a benefit of $2,160 would be paid.

But, of course, if no other government subsidy were paid to the family (and the original NIT sponsors proposed that their plan be a complete *substitute* for all other welfare payments) then the government would be paying the poorest families only *half* of what its own administrators officially declared to be the *minimum* on which such families could reasonably be expected to live. How could such a program be politically defended?

As soon as the NIT program gets into practical politics, therefore, the pressure will be irresistible to make the payment to a family with zero income at least equal to the official poverty line income. If this means $4,320 for a family of four, say, then *some* NIT payment must be made to each family until its income reaches *twice* the official poverty line income, or $8,640 for every family of four. And this means that even if a family were already earning much more than the official poverty line income—say, $8,000 a year—it would still have to be subsidized by the government. "Everybody must be treated alike."

4. This would be ruinously expensive, but it is still not the end. The subsidized families would object to paying a 50 percent income tax (as their spokesmen would put it) on everything they earned for themselves. So they would be allowed to earn a certain amount entirely exempted from such a deduction. (Such an exemption has already been granted on self-earnings of Social Security recipients, and a similar exemption has been proposed in Congressional bills to enact an NIT.) This would make the NIT still more crushingly expensive for the remaining taxpayers.

5. There would be political pressures every year for increasing the amount of these exempted earnings. In fact, a 50 percent "income tax on the poor" would be denounced as an outrage. In time the proposal would be certain to be made that *all* the self-earnings of the NIT subsidy recipients be exempted from any offsetting deductions whatever. But this would mean that once a family had been granted the initial minimum income guarantee of, say, $4,320 a year, it would still be getting that full sum in addition to whatever it earned for itself. But "everybody must be treated alike." Therefore there would be no break-off point, or even any tapering off. Every family—including the Rockefellers, the Fords, the Gettys, and all the other millionaires—would get the full guaranteed income.

This end result cannot be dismissed as mere fantasy. The

principle of a government subsidy to any family, no matter how rich, is already accepted in our own Social Security scheme. And Senator George McGovern, running for President in 1972, proposed a $1,000-a-year government gift to everybody, man, woman, or child, with no tapering-off point. So the Negative Income Tax, as a social measure, turns out to be only a halfway house. When its logic is carried out unswervingly, it becomes a uniform guaranteed handout to industrious and idle, thrifty and improvident, poor and rich alike.

6. It is an anticlimax to point out (but it needs to be done) that there is no political possibility that a flat guaranteed income or a "negative income tax" would be enacted as a complete *substitute* for the existing jumble of welfare and relief measures. Can we seriously imagine that the specific pressure groups now getting veterans' allowances, farm subsidies, rent subsidies, relief payments, Social Security benefits, food stamps, Medicare, Medicaid, old-age assistance, unemployment insurance, and so on and so on, would quietly give them up, without protests, demonstrations, or riots? The overwhelming probability is that a guaranteed income or NIT program would simply be thrown on top of the whole present rag-bag of welfare measures piled up over the last thirty to forty years.

We may put it down as a political law that all State handout schemes tend to grow and grow until they bring on hyperinflation and finally bankrupt the State.

"Land Reform"

Perhaps I should devote at least one or two paragraphs here to so-called "land reform." This appears to be the most ancient of schemes for forcibly dividing the wealth. In 133 B.C., for example, Tiberius Gracchus succeeded in getting a law passed in Rome severely limiting the number of acres that any one person could possess. The typical "land reform" since his day, repeatedly adopted in backward agricultural countries, has consisted in confiscating the big estates and either "collectivizing" them or breaking them up into small plots and redistributing these among the peasants. Because there are always fewer such workable parcels than families, and because, though each parcel of land may be of the same nominal acreage, each has a different nature, fertility, location, and degree of development (with or without clearance, grading, irrigation, roads, buildings, etc.), each must have a different market value. The distribution of land can never be universal and can never be "fair"; it must necessarily favor a selected group, and some more than others within that group.

But apart from all this, such a measure always reduces efficiency and production. From the moment it is proposed that property be seized, its owners "mine" its fertility and refuse to invest another dollar in it, and some may not even raise another crop. It does not pay to use modern equipment on small farms, and in any case the owners are unlikely to have the necessary capital. "Land reform" of this type is an impoverishment measure.

The Henry George scheme of a 100 percent "single tax" on ground rent would also discourage the most productive utilization of land and sites, and adversely affect general economic development. But to explain adequately why this is so would require so lengthy an exposition that I must refer the interested reader to the excellent analyses that have already been made by Rothbard, Knight, and others.[4]

Progressive Income Taxes

Among the "advanced" nations of the West, however, the most frequent contemporary method of redistributing income

4. Murray C. Rothbard, *Power and Market: Government and the Economy*, Menlo Park: Institute for Humane Studies, Inc., 1970, pp. 91–100; Frank H. Knight, "The Fallacies in the 'Single Tax,'" *The Freeman*, August 10, 1953.

and wealth is through progressive income and inheritance taxes. These now commonly rise to near-confiscatory levels. A recent compilation[5] comparing the highest marginal income-tax rates in fifteen countries yielded the following results: Switzerland, 8 percent; Norway, 50; Denmark, 53; West Germany, 55; Sweden, 65; Belgium, 66; Australia, 68; Austria, 69; Netherlands, 71; Japan, 75; France, 76; United States, 77; Canada, 82; United Kingdom, 91; and Italy, 95 percent.

Two main points may be made about these hyper-rates: (1) they do not raise much revenue, but (2) they do hurt not only the rich but the poor, and tend to make them poorer.

All the revenues yielded by the U.S. personal income tax of 1968, with its rates ranging from 14 to 70 percent, plus a 10 percent surcharge, would have been yielded, with the same exemptions and deductions, by a flat income tax of 21.8 percent. If all the tax rates above 50 percent had been reduced to that level, the loss would not have been as much as it took to run the government for a full day. In Great Britain, in the fiscal year 1964–65, the revenue from all the surtax rates (ranging above the standard rate of 41¼ percent up to 96¼ percent) yielded less than 6 percent of all the revenue from the income tax, and barely more than 2 percent of total revenues. In Sweden, in 1963, the rates between 45 and 65 percent brought in only 1 percent of the total national income-tax revenue. And so it goes. The great masses of the people are accepting far higher rates of income tax than they would tolerate if it were not for their *illusion* that the very rich are footing the greater part of the bill.

One effect of seizing so high a percentage of high earnings is to diminish or remove the incentive to bring such earnings into existence in the first place. It is very difficult to estimate this effect in quantitative terms, because we are comparing actualities merely with might-be's and might-have-been's. In March,

5. First National City Bank of New York.

1947, the National City Bank, based on reports of the Bureau of Internal Revenue, presented the illuminating table below.

	1926–28 Average (in millions)	1942 Average (in millions)
National Income	$77,000	$122,000
Incomes over $300,000:		
Total amount	$ 1,669	$376
Taxes paid	$ 281	$292
Top tax rate applicable	25%	88%
Number of returns	2,276	654

In other words, during the same period in which the total national income *increased* 58 percent, total incomes over $300,-000 *fell* 77 percent. If the aggregate of such $300,000 incomes had risen proportionately to the whole national income, the total would have reached $2,644 million—seven times greater than it actually was.

A great deal more statistical analysis of this sort could instructively be undertaken not only from U.S. but from many foreign income-tax returns.

But it is not merely the effect of personal and corporate income taxes in reducing the incentives to bring high earnings into existence that needs to be considered, but their total effect in soaking up the sources of capital funds. Most of the funds that the present tax structure now seizes for current government expenditures are precisely those that would have gone principally into investment—i.e., into improved machines and new plants to provide the increased per capita productivity which is the only permanent and continuous means of increasing wages and total national wealth and income. In the long run, the high rates of personal and corporate income taxes hurt the poor more than the rich.

Equality, Once for All

A socialist proposal that used to be aired frequently a generation or two ago but is not much heard now (when the emphasis is on trying to legislate permanent equalization of incomes) is that the wealth of the country ought to be distributed equally "once for all," so as to give everybody an even start. But Irving Fisher pointed out in answer that this equality could not long endure.[6] It is not merely that everybody would continue to earn different incomes as the result of differences in ability, industry, and luck, but differences in thrift alone would soon reestablish inequality. Society would still be divided into "spenders" and "savers." One man would quickly go into debt to spend his money on luxuries and immediate pleasures; another would save and invest present income for the sake of future income. "It requires only a very small degree of saving or spending to lead to comparative wealth or poverty, even in one generation."

Even Communists have now learned that wealth and income cannot be created merely by alluring slogans and utopian dreams. As no less a figure than Leonid I. Brezhnev, First Secretary of the Soviet Communist Party, recently put it at a Party Congress in Moscow: "One can only distribute and consume what has been produced; this is an elementary truth."[7] What the Communists have still to learn, however, is that the institution of capitalism, of private property and free markets, tends to maximize production, while economic dictatorship and forced redistribution only discourage, reduce, and disrupt it.

6. Irving Fisher, *Elementary Principles of Economics,* New York: Macmillan, 1921, pp. 478–483.
7. *The New York Times,* May 29, 1971.

CHAPTER 12

On Appeasing Envy

ANY ATTEMPT TO EQUALIZE WEALTH OR INCOME BY FORCED REDISTRI-bution must only tend to destroy wealth and income. Histori-cally the best the would-be equalizers have ever succeeded in doing is to equalize downward. This has even been caustically described as their intention. "Your levellers," said Samuel Johnson in the mid-eighteenth century, "wish to level *down* as far as themselves; but they cannot bear levelling *up* to them-selves." And in our own day we find even an eminent liberal like the late Mr. Justice Holmes writing: "I have no respect for the passion for equality, which seems to me merely idealizing envy."[1]

At least a handful of writers have begun to recognize explic-itly the all-pervasive role played by envy or the fear of envy in life and in contemporary political thought. In 1966, Helmut Schoeck, professor of sociology at the University of Mainz, de-

1. M. de Wolfe Howe, ed., *The Correspondence of Mr. Justice Holmes and Harold J. Laski*, 2 vol., Cambridge, Mass., 1953. From Holmes to Laski, May 12, 1927, p. 942.

voted a scholarly and penetrating book to the subject, to which most future discussion is likely to be indebted.[2]

There can be little doubt that many egalitarians are motivated at least partly by envy, while still others are motivated, not so much by any envy of their own, as by the fear of it in others, and the wish to appease or satisfy it.

But the latter effort is bound to be futile. Almost no one is completely satisfied with his status in relation to his fellows. In the envious the thirst for social advancement is insatiable. As soon as they have risen one rung in the social or economic ladder, their eyes are fixed upon the next. They envy those who are higher up, no matter by how little. In fact, they are more likely to envy their immediate friends or neighbors, who are just a little bit better off, than celebrities or millionaires who are incomparably better off. The position of the latter seems unattainable, but of the neighbor who has just a minimal advantage they are tempted to think: "I might almost be in his place."

Moreover, the envious are more likely to be mollified by seeing others deprived of some advantage than by gaining it for themselves. It is not what they lack that chiefly troubles them, but what others have. The envious are not satisfied with equality; they secretly yearn for superiority and revenge. In the French Revolution of 1848, a woman coal-heaver is said to have remarked to a richly dressed lady: "Yes, madam, everything's going to be equal now; I shall go in silks and you'll carry coal."

Envy is implacable. Concessions merely whet its appetite for more concessions. As Schoeck writes: "Man's envy is at its most intense where all are almost equal; his calls for redistribution are loudest when there is virtually nothing to redistribute."[3]

(We should, of course, always distinguish that merely nega-

2. Helmut Schoeck, *Envy*, English tr., Harcourt, Brace & World, 1969.
3. *Ibid.*, p. 303.

tive envy which begrudges others their advantage from the positive ambition that leads men to active emulation, competition, and creative effort of their own.)

But the accusation of envy, or even of the fear of others' envy, as the dominant motive for any redistribution proposal is a serious one to make and a difficult if not impossible one to prove. Moreover, the motives for making a proposal, even if ascertainable, are irrelevant to its inherent merits. We can, nonetheless, apply certain objective tests. Sometimes the motive of appeasing other people's envy is openly avowed. Socialists will often talk as if some form of superbly equalized destitution were preferable to "maldistributed" plenty. A national income that is rapidly growing in absolute terms for practically everyone will be deplored because it is making the rich richer. An implied and sometimes avowed principle of the British Labor Party leaders after World War II was that "Nobody should have what everybody can't have."

But the main objective test of a social proposal is not merely whether it emphasizes equality more than abundance, but whether it goes further and attempts to promote equality at the expense of abundance. Is the proposed measure intended primarily to help the poor, or to penalize the rich? And would it in fact punish the rich at the cost of also hurting everyone else?

This is the actual effect, as we saw in the last chapter, of steeply progressive income taxes and confiscatory inheritance taxes. These are not only counterproductive fiscally (bringing in less revenue from the higher brackets than lower rates would have brought), but they discourage or confiscate the capital accumulation and investment that would have increased national productivity and real wages. Most of the confiscated funds are then dissipated by the government in current consumption expenditures. The long-run effect of such tax rates, of course, is to leave the working poor worse off than they would otherwise have been.

There are economists who will admit all this, but will answer that it is nonetheless politically necessary to impose such near-confiscatory taxes, or to enact similar redistributive measures, in order to placate the dissatisfied and the envious—in order, in fact, to prevent actual revolution.

This argument is the reverse of the truth. The effect of trying to appease envy is to provoke more of it.

The most popular theory of the French Revolution is that it came about because the economic condition of the masses was becoming worse and worse, while the king and the aristocracy remained completely blind to it. But de Tocqueville, one of the most penetrating social observers and historians of his or any other time, put forward an exactly opposite explanation. Let me state it first as summarized by an eminent French commentator in 1899:

"Here is the theory invented by Tocqueville. . . . The lighter a yoke, the more it seems insupportable; what exasperates is not the crushing burden but the impediment; what inspires to revolt is not oppression but humiliation. The French of 1789 were incensed against the nobles because they were *almost* the equals of the nobles; it is the slight difference that can be appreciated, and what can be appreciated that counts. The eighteenth-century middle class was rich, in a position to fill *almost* any employment, *almost* as powerful as the nobility. It was exasperated by this *"almost"* and stimulated by the proximity of its goal; impatience is always provoked by the final strides."[4]

I have quoted this passage because I do not find the theory stated in quite this condensed form by Tocqueville himself. Yet this is essentially the theme of his *L'Ancien Régime et la Révolution,* and he presented impressive factual documentation to support it. Here is a typical passage:

4. Emile Faguet, *Politicians and Moralists of the Nineteenth Century,* Boston: Little, Brown; 1928, p. 93.

It is a singular fact that this steadily increasing prosperity, far from tranquilizing the population, everywhere promoted a spirit of unrest. The general public became more and more hostile to every ancient institution, more and more discontented; indeed, it was increasingly obvious that the nation was heading for a revolution. . . .

Thus it was precisely in those parts of France where there had been most improvement that popular discontent ran highest. This may seem illogical—but history is full of such paradoxes. For it is not always when things are going from bad to worse that revolutions break out. On the contrary, it oftener happens that when a people which has put up with an oppressive rule over a long period without protest suddenly finds the government relaxing its pressure, it takes up arms against it. Thus the social order overthrown by a revolution is almost always better than the one immediately preceding it, and experience teaches us that, generally speaking, the most perilous moment for a bad government is one when it seeks to mend its ways. Only consummate statecraft can enable a King to save his throne when after a long spell of oppressive rule he sets to improving the lot of his subjects. Patiently endured so long as it seemed beyond redress, a grievance comes to appear intolerable once the possibility of removing it crosses men's minds. For the mere fact that certain abuses have been remedied draws attention to the others and they now appear more galling; people may suffer less, but their sensibility is exacerbated. . . .

In 1780 there could no longer be any talk of France's being on the downgrade; on the contrary, it seemed that no limit could be set to her advance. And it was now that theories of the perfectibility of man and continuous progress came into fashion. Twenty years earlier there had been no hope for the future; in 1780 no anxiety was felt about it. Dazzled by the prospect of a felicity undreamed of hitherto and now within their grasp, people were blind to the very improvement that had taken place and eager to precipitate events.[5]

The expressions of sympathy that came from the privileged class only aggravated the situation:

The very men who had most to fear from the anger of the masses had no qualms about publicly condemning the gross injustice with

5. Alexis de Tocqueville, *The Old Regime and the French Revolution*, Doubleday Anchor Books, 1955, pp. 175–177.

which they had always been treated. They drew attention to the monstrous vices of the institutions which pressed most heavily on the common people and indulged in highly colored descriptions of the living conditions of the working class and the starvation wages it received. And thus by championing the cause of the underprivileged they made them acutely conscious of their wrongs."[6]

Tocqueville went on to quote at length from the mutual recriminations of the king, the nobles, and the parliament in blaming each other for the miseries of the people. To read them now is to get the uncanny feeling that they are plagiarizing the rhetoric of the limousine liberals of our own day.

All this does not mean that we should hesitate to take any measure truly calculated to relieve hardship and reduce poverty. What it does mean is that we should never take governmental measures merely for the purpose of trying to assuage the envious or appease the agitators, or to buy off a revolution. Such measures, betraying weakness and a guilty conscience, only lead to more far-reaching and even ruinous demands. A government that pays social blackmail will precipitate the very consequences that it fears.

6. *Ibid.,* p. 180.

CHAPTER 13

How Unions Reduce Real Wages

FOR MORE THAN A CENTURY THE ECONOMIC THINKING NOT ONLY OF the public but of the majority of economists has been dominated by a myth—the myth that labor unions have been on the whole a highly beneficent institution, and have raised the level of real wages far above what it would have been without union pressure. Many even talk as if the unions had been chiefly responsible for whatever gains labor has made.

Yet the blunt truth is that labor unions cannot raise the real wages of all workers. We may go further: the actual policies that labor unions have systematically followed from the beginning of their existence have in fact reduced the real wages of the workers as a whole below what they would otherwise have been. Labor unions are today the chief antilabor force.

To realize why this is so we must understand what determines wages in a free market. Wage rates are prices. Like other prices they are determined by supply and demand. And the demand for labor is determined by the marginal productivity of labor.

If wage rates go above that level, employers drop their marginal workers because it costs more to employ them than they earn. They cannot long be employed at a loss. If, on the other hand, wage rates fall below the marginal productivity of workers, employers bid against each other for more workers up to the point where there is no further marginal profit in hiring more or bidding up wages more.

So assuming mobility of both capital and labor, assuming free competition between workers and free competition between employers, there would be full employment of every person wanting and able to work, and the wage rate of each would tend to equal his marginal productivity.

It will be said—it has in fact repeatedly been said—that such an analysis is merely a beautiful abstraction and that in the actual world this mobility and competition of labor and capital do not exist. There is, some economists have argued, in fact a wide range of "indeterminacy" in wages, and it is the function of unions to make sure that wage rates are fixed at the top rather than the bottom of this range or zone.

We cannot reply that this indeterminacy theory is wholly wrong; but what we can say is that in relation to the problem of unions it is unimportant. The indeterminacy theory is true of wages only to the extent that it is true of other prices: it is true where the market is narrow or specialized. It is true, say, of highly specialized jobs in journalism, or in the universities, or in scientific research, or in the professions. But wherever we have large numbers of unskilled workers, or large numbers of approximately equal special but widespread skills—such as carpenters, bricklayers, painters, plumbers, printers, trainmen, truckdrivers—this zone of indeterminacy shrinks or disappears. It is the craft unions themselves who insist that their individual members are so nearly equal to each other in competence that all should be paid on equal "standard" wage. And so we have the paradox that the unions exist and flourish precisely where they are least necessary to assure that their members get a market wage equal to their marginal productivity.

It is true, of course, that an individual union can succeed in forcing the money wage rates of its members above what the free market rate would be. It can do this through the device of a strike, or often merely through the threat of a strike.

Now a strike is not, as it is constantly represented as being, merely the act of a worker in "withholding his labor," or even merely a collusion of a large group of workers *simultaneously* to "withhold their labor" or give up their jobs. The whole point of a strike is the insistence by the strikers that they have not given up their jobs at all. They contend that they are still employees—in fact, the only legitimate employees. They claim an *ownership* of the jobs at which they refuse to work; they claim the "right" to prevent anybody else from taking the jobs that they have abandoned. That is the purpose of their mass picket lines, and of the vandalism and violence that they either resort to or threaten. They insist that the employer has no right to replace them with other workers, temporary or permanent, and they mean to see to it that he doesn't. Their demands are enforced always by intimidation and coercion, and in the last resort by actual violence.

So wherever a union makes a gain by a strike or strike threat, it makes it by forcibly excluding other workers from taking the jobs that the strikers have abandoned. The union always makes its gains at the expense of these excluded workers.

Overlooking the Victims

It is amazing to find how systematically the self-proclaimed humanitarians, even among professional economists, have managed to overlook the unemployed, or the still more poorly paid workers, who are the victims of the union members' "gains."

It is important to keep in mind that the unions cannot create a "monopoly" of all labor, but at best a monopoly of labor in certain specific crafts, firms, or industries. A monopolist of a product can get a higher monopoly price for that product, and perhaps a higher total income from it, by deliberately restricting the supply, either by refusing to produce as much as he can of it, or by withholding part of it, or even by destroying part of it that has already come into existence. But while the unions can and do restrict their membership, and exclude other workers from it, they cannot reduce the total number of workers seeking jobs.

Therefore whenever the unions gain higher wage rates for their own members than free competition would have brought, they can do this only by increasing unemployment, or by increasing the number of workers forced to compete for other jobs and so comparatively reducing the wage rates paid for such jobs. All union "gains" (i.e., wage rates above what a competitive free market would have brought) are at the expense of lower wages than otherwise for at least some if not most nonunion workers. The unions cannot raise the average level of real wages; they can at best distort it.

As the gains of union workers are made at the expense of nonunion workers, it is instructive to ask what proportion union members constitute of the whole working population. The answer for the United States is that union members now number about 20 million, or not more than 25 percent of the total civilian labor force of 87 million. So the unions are in a distinct minority. This might not be a fact worth emphasizing if there were reason to think that the average earnings of union workers were below the average earnings of nonunion workers. But while statistical comparisons cannot be exact, the evidence is conclusive that the case is the other way round. It is the most skilled occupations that are most unionized. In brief, we have a one-quarter minority of already higher paid union workers exploiting a three-quarters majority consisting mainly of already lower paid nonunion workers.

People could save themselves a good deal of misplaced sympathy if next time they read in their newspapers of a strike for a "decent wage," they take the trouble to compare what the strikers were already getting with, say, the official statistics of average wages for all nonagricultural workers.

The "gains" of union labor, of course, need not be solely at the expense of nonunion labor; they may be at the expense of some union members themselves. The higher wage rates gained in a particular industry (assuming an elastic demand for its product) will lead to less employment than otherwise in that industry. This may force unemployment on some of the members of the "successful" union. The result may then be that smaller *aggregate* wages will be paid in that industry than if the higher wage rate had not been successfully imposed.

In addition, any union's "gains" (continuing to use "gains" in the sense of any excess over what would have been free-market wage rates) will be at the expense not only of unemployment or lower pay for other workers, but at the expense of consumers, by forcing them to pay higher prices. But as the great bulk of consumers consists of *other workers,* this means that these gains will be at the expense not only of nonunion workers but also of other *union* workers. The real wages of the mass of workers are reduced whenever they have to pay higher prices.

Once it is clearly recognized that the strike-threat gains of each union are at the expense of all other unions, in forcing their members to pay higher prices for products, the whole myth of "labor solidarity" collapses. It is this myth that has kept the strike-threat system going. It has created sympathy for strikes and tolerance of the public harm they do. The mass of the working population has been taught to believe that all workers should support every strike, no matter how disorderly or for what unreasonable demands, and always to "respect the picket lines," because "Labor's" interests are unified. The success of any strike is thought to help all labor and its failure to hurt all labor.

The Great Illusion

This is the modern Great Illusion. In fact, each union's extorted "gains," by raising a specific industry's costs and therefore its prices, reduces the real wages of all other workers. The interests of the unions are mutually antagonistic.

I have been talking so far about the damage done by strike settlements, or by "gains" extorted under the threat of strikes; I have not yet talked about the damage done by the strike itself. While strikes are ostensibly directed against the employers, most of them are in fact directed against the public. The idea is that if enough hardship is inflicted on the public, then the public will insist that the employer capitulate to the strikers' demands.

There are too many instances of this to list. For examples one need not go outside of New York City in recent years. A bus and subway strike. A strike of garbage collectors, bringing filth, stench, and the threat of an epidemic. A strike in late December, 1968, of fuel-oil deliverers and oil-burner repairmen, during an extreme cold spell and flu epidemic, when at least 40,000 persons in thousands of multiple dwellings were reported to be seriously ill and were deprived of heat. A strike of 20,000 employees of the Consolidated Edison Co., which supplies the electric power for New York. Grave-diggers' strikes. Hospital employees' strikes.

The chief leverage of the strikers, in securing capitulation to their demands, was the amount of hardship and suffering they were able to inflict, not directly on the employers, but primarily on the public. Yet who are the public? They are in the main other workers, including other union members. They may even be members of the striking union itself and of their families. A striking fuel oil deliverer's own children, for example, may be sick and shivering because no fuel has been delivered.

This is the absurdity of "labor solidarity." This is the folly of

136

a "general strike." Such a strike is suicidal for the workers themselves.

This is a war of each against all. The minute division of labor in our modern industrial society, which makes our society so productive, also makes it increasingly interdependent. So each of hundreds of unions successively tries to exploit the community's dependence on that type of worker's special services and on the harm it can do by withholding them and preventing anybody else from supplying them. A huge motor truck can be brought to a halt if someone removes either the carburetor, or the distributor, or the battery, or a single wheel, or even disconnects a single tiny wire. In the same way the industry of a country can be brought to a halt while the workers in a single small branch proudly demonstrate the indispensability of that branch's specialized services.

But how could it have come to be seriously believed that this disorderly, haphazard, violent, extortionate, obstructive, piecemeal, every-union-for-itself scrimmage is the way to promote "social justice?" So far from the strike-threat system promoting cooperation within the "labor movement," each union leader, to hold his job, tries to prove that he can get more for the members of his particular union than others can get for their unions. This is a competition in leap-frogging, with each union trying to end up as the one on top of the heap.

I have yet to see any serious or self-consistent exposition anywhere of the union theory of wage formation. I have yet to hear any union apologist, for example, try to determine scientifically exactly how much the members of a particular union are being underpaid, how much of an increase they are justified in demanding, and how much would be too much. The union leaders have one simple formula for every situation: More.

Insofar as they do have an implied theory it seems to be some obscure form of the Marxist exploitation dogma. They never suggest that wages can be rightly determined in a free market. The employer, one gathers, never voluntarily pays what is "fair," but raises wages only in response to a strike threat or "tough bargaining" on the part of the union leaders. And the gains that the union wins for its members are solely at the expense of the employer and of his "excess profits." The gains of the workers simply leave less for the capitalists.

Now this can indeed be true in a particular industry and for the short run. When capital has already been invested in a particular industry, in expensive specialized plant or heavy equipment—say in a railroad, a steel plant, or an automobile plant—that capital is locked in—is held hostage, so to speak—and it is possible for unions to exploit it. The plant will continue to be operated, and to employ labor, as long as it can still earn anything above running expenses, regardless of how little it yields on already invested capital. But new fixed capital will not be invested in that plant or industry, at least not until it can once more earn as much return as new capital invested elsewhere. Meanwhile that industry will not expand, or will actually shrink, and employment in it will decline.

Discouraging Capital Investment

This result will follow not only because of the success of previous strikes or strike threats in that particular industry. When strike threats have become chronic in an industry, and seem likely to be systematically repeated, new capital and new investment will no longer venture into that industry. Union tactics may even end by discouraging and gravely reducing new investment everywhere.

Hence the strike gains of unions are at best short-run gains. In the long run they not only reduce employment but reduce the real wages of the whole body of workers. For the productivity of industry—and the real wages of workers—are dependent on the amount of investment of capital per head of the working population. It is only because American manufacturing industry has invested more than industry in any other country—

some $30,000 for every production worker[1]—that American wages so greatly exceed wages in any other country.

Labor unions can only exploit capital already invested, and they can do this only at the cost of discouraging new investment. By discouraging new investment, by discouraging maintenance, expansion, and modernization, labor unions in the long run reduce real wages below what they would otherwise have been.

But this is not the only way in which labor unions reduce real wages. They do so, and they have done so since the beginning of their existence, by jurisdictional disputes, by forcing the employment of more workers than are necessary for a particular job, by systematic hostility to piecework, by forcing slowdowns, soldiering and malingering on the excuse that they are combatting unreasonable speed-ups, and by countless other featherbedding practices.

In a famous review of William Thornton's book on labor, John Stuart Mill wrote in 1869:

"Some of the Unionist regulations go even further than to prohibit improvements; they are contrived for the express purpose of making work inefficient; they positively prohibit the workman from working hard and well, in order that it may be necessary to employ a greater number. Regulations that no one shall move bricks in a wheelbarrow, but only carry them in a hod, and then no more than eight at a time; that stones shall not be worked at the quarry while they are soft, but must be worked by the masons at the place where they are to be used; that the plasterers shall not do the work of plasterers' laborers, nor laborers that of plasterers, but a plasterer and a laborer must both be employed when one would suffice; that bricks made on one side of a particular canal must lie there unused, while fresh bricks are made for work going on upon the other; that men shall not do so good a day's work as to 'best their mates';

1. Estimate for 1968 by The Conference Board, "Road Map to Industry," No. 1676.

139

that they shall not walk at more than a given pace to their work when the walk is counted 'in the master's time'—these and scores of similar examples . . . will be found in Mr. Thornton's book."

These depressingly familiar practices, in short, have been going on for more than a century. The unions, far from "maturing," show not the slightest sign of abandoning them, but create more unreasonable obstacles than ever, still combat the introduction of labor-saving machinery, refuse to accept discipline, and undermine more and more management's ability to manage.

To reduce productivity is to reduce wages. These shortsighted practices can only have the long-run effect of keeping real wages far below that they could otherwise be.

Unions and Inflation

It remains to say a word about the effect of unions on inflation. Contrary to a widespread opinion, unions do not directly cause inflation by using strikes or strike threats to force wage rate increases. The normal economic result of such excessive wage rate increases would simply be to wipe out profit margins and create unemployment. But under the influence of Keynesian ideology and present political pressures, it is assumed to be the duty of the monetary authorities to issue more money to raise prices to make the higher wages possible and payable. As long as this ideology lasts, wage increases forced by unions will lead to progressive inflation. This process must eventually collapse, with disastrous consequences. Meanwhile, by forcing faster increases in money wage rates, it further promotes the popular illusion that unions raise real wages.

I have hitherto not explicitly mentioned a very important point which consistently escapes the Keynesians and all union apologists. A distinction that must be constantly kept in mind is that between wage *rates* and *total payrolls* or aggregate

140

wage *income*. Whenever higher wage rates lead to more than proportionate unemployment they reduce labor's total income. Therefore such forced wage rate increases are not a gain for labor but a loss for labor. But the union leaders and the union apologists put all their emphasis on winning higher wage rates.

To sum up. The net overall effect of union policy has historically been to reduce productivity, to discourage new investment, to slow down capital formation, to distort the structure and balance of production, to drive nonunion members into lower paid jobs, and to reduce the total production and the total real wages and real income of the whole body of workers below what it would otherwise have been.

The rates of wages that are best for the workers as a whole are those that are determined in a free market.

There are, no doubt, areas in which the activities of unions, wisely directed, could be on the whole beneficent—in negotiating with individual employers, for example, concerning hours of work and such conditions of work as light, air, sanitary arrangements, rest rooms, coffee breaks, shop rules, grievance machinery, and the like. But wherever the unions are allowed to use violence and coercive tactics to achieve any aim, the long-run result is bound to be bad for the workers themselves.

This being so, what should be the public's attitude toward labor unions, and what should be the legal framework in which they operate?

The public must recognize, first of all, that the interests of unions and union leaders are by no means identical with the interests of labor as a whole, and that being pro-union is by no means synonymous with being pro-labor.

In accordance with the principle of freedom of peaceful association, the law should not prohibit unions, but neither should it go out of its way to encourage them. Certainly the government should not continue, as it does in the United States, to turn itself in effect into a union-organizing agency and to force employers to negotiate with unions. And under no conditions should the law—or the law-enforcement officials—tolerate union violence, vandalism, or intimidation.

To translate this into more concrete terms: American Federal, state and city governments need not forbid unions of their own employees, but neither should they have any obligation to recognize, consult, or negotiate with such unions in fixing compensation or conditions of work. Under no conditions should they tolerate a strike by public employees. Public officials have been notoriously spineless in dealing with unions, but the law should give them wide discretion in deciding what penalties to impose, from loss of pay and mild fines to suspension or permanent dismissal. None of these penalties will be effective, of course, unless public officials also have a clear right to hire immediately temporary or permanent replacements for the strikers.

For private industry the minimum need is (1) the complete repeal of the Norris-LaGuardia Act of 1932—which in effect denies injunctive relief during a strike to employers and nonstrikers from violence, vandalism, and intimidation—and (2) the repeal of the Wagner-Taft-Hartley Act of 1935 and 1947— which compels employers to recognize and "bargain collectively with" specified unions, and in effect make concessions to them.

Repeal of these and other laws would merely return the United States to the pre-1932 Federal legal situation. In addition, however, all mass picketing should be forbidden, as well as any picketing whatever that involves harassment or intimidation.

The century-old tolerance on the part of public officials of union coercion and violence is in large part a product of the myth that such violence is necessary to secure "fair wages" and "justice for labor." Not until this myth is destroyed can we hope to have industrial peace, orderly economic progress, and maximum real income for the great body of the workers.

CHAPTER 14

False Remedies for Poverty

FROM THE BEGINNING OF HISTORY SINCERE REFORMERS AS WELL AS demagogues have sought to abolish or at least to alleviate poverty through state action. In most cases their proposed remedies have only served to make the problem worse.

The most frequent and popular of these proposed remedies has been the simple one of seizing from the rich to give to the poor. This remedy has taken a thousand different forms, but they all come down to this. The wealth is to be "shared," to be "redistributed," to be "equalized." In fact, in the minds of many reformers it is not poverty that is the chief evil but inequality.

These direct redistribution schemes (including "land reform" and "the guaranteed income") are so immediately relevant to the problem of poverty that I have treated them separately in Chapter 11. Here I need merely remind the reader that all schemes for redistributing or equalizing incomes or wealth must undermine or destroy incentives at both ends of the economic scale. They must reduce or abolish the incentives of the unskilled or shiftless to improve their condition by their own efforts; and even the able and industrious will see little point in earning anything beyond what they are allowed to keep. These redistribution schemes must inevitably reduce the size of the pie to be redistributed. They can only level down. Their long-run effect must be to reduce production and lead toward national impoverishment.

The problem we face in the present chapter is that the false remedies for poverty are almost infinite in number. An attempt at a thorough refutation of any single one of them would run to disproportionate length. But some of these false remedies are so widely regarded as real cures or mitigations of poverty that if I do not refer to them I may be accused of having undertaken a book on the remedies for poverty while ignoring some of the most obvious.

What I shall do, as a compromise, is to take up some of the more popular of the alleged remedies for poverty and indicate briefly in each case the nature of their shortcomings or the chief fallacies involved in them.[1]

The most widely practiced "remedy" for low incomes in the last two centuries has been the formation of monopolistic labor unions and the use of the strike threat. In nearly every country today this has been made possible to its present extent by government policies that permit and encourage coercive union tactics and inhibit or restrict counter actions by employers. I have dealt with this in the preceding chapter. As a result of union exclusiveness, of deliberate inefficiency, of featherbedding, of disruptive strikes and strike threats, the long-run effect of customary union policies, as we saw, has been to discourage capital investment and to make the average real wage of the whole body of workers lower, and not higher, than it would otherwise have been.

Nearly all of these customary union policies have been dis-

1. I have examined most of these schemes in more detail elsewhere (chiefly in my *Economics in One Lesson* and in *Man vs. the Welfare State*) and must refer the interested reader to these and other sources for more extended discussion.

hearteningly shortsighted. When unions insist on the employment of men who are not necessary to do a job (requiring unneeded firemen on diesel locomotives; forbidding the gang size of dock workers to be reduced below, say, twenty men no matter what the size of the task; demanding that a newspaper's own printers must duplicate advertising copy that comes in already set in type, etc.), the result may be to preserve or create a few more jobs for specific men in the short run, but only at the cost of making impossible the creation of an equivalent or greater number of more productive jobs for others.

The same criticism applies to the age-old union policy of opposing the use of labor-saving machinery. Labor-saving machinery is installed only when it promises to reduce production costs. When it does that, it either reduces prices and leads to increased production and sales of the commodity being produced, or it makes more profits available for increased reinvestment in other production. In either case its long-run effect is to substitute more productive jobs for the less productive jobs it eliminates. Yet as late as 1970, a book appeared by a writer who enjoys a lofty reputation as an economist in some quarters, opposing the introduction of labor-saving machines in the underdeveloped countries on the ground that they "decrease the demand for labor"![2] The logical conclusion from this would be that the way to maximize jobs is to make all labor as inefficient and unproductive as possible.

A similar judgment must be passed on all "spread-the-work" schemes. The existing Federal Wage-Hour Law has been on the books for many years. It provides that the employer must pay a 50 percent penalty overtime rate for all hours that an employee works in excess of 40 hours a week, no matter how high the employee's standard hourly rate of pay.

This provision was inserted at the insistence of the unions. Its purpose was to make it so costly for the employer to work men overtime that he would be obliged to take on additional workers.

2. Gunnar Myrdal, *The Challenge of World Poverty,* Pantheon Books, 1970, pp. 400–401 and *passim.*

Experience shows that the provision has in fact had the effect of narrowly restricting the length of the working week. In the ten-year period 1962 to 1971 inclusive, the average annual work-week in manufacturing varied only between a low of 39.8 hours in 1970 and a high of 41.3 hours in 1966. Even monthly changes do not show much variation. The lowest average working week in manufacturing in the fourteen months from June, 1971, to July, 1972, was 39.8 hours and the highest was 40.9 hours.

But it does not follow that the hour restriction either created more long-term jobs or yielded higher total payrolls than would have existed without the compulsory 50 percent overtime rate. No doubt in isolated cases more men have been employed than would otherwise have been. But the chief effect of the overtime law has been to raise production costs. Firms already working full standard time often have to refuse new orders because they cannot afford to pay the penalty overtime necessary to fill those orders. They cannot afford to take on new employees to meet what may be only a temporarily higher demand because they may also have to install an equivalent number of additional machines.

Higher production costs mean higher prices. They must therefore mean narrowed markets and smaller sales. They mean that fewer goods and services are produced. In the long run the interests of the whole body of workers must be adversely affected by compulsory overtime penalties.

All this is not to argue that there ought to be a longer work week, but rather that the length of the work week, and the scale of overtime rates, ought to be left to voluntary agreement between individual workers or unions and their employers. In any case, legal restrictions on the length of the working week cannot in the long run increase the number of jobs. To the extent that they can do that in the short run, it must necessarily be at the expense of production and of the real income of the whole body of workers.

Minimum-Wage Laws

This brings us to the subject of minimum-wage laws. It is profoundly discouraging that in the second half of the twentieth century, in what is supposed to be an age of great economic sophistication, the United States should have such laws on its books, and that it should still be necessary to protest against a remedy so futile and mischievous. It hurts most the very marginal workers it is designed to help.

I can only repeat what I have written in another place.[3] When a law exists that no one is to be paid less than $64 for a 40-hour week, then no one whose services are not worth $64 a week to an employer will be employed at all. We cannot make a man worth a given amount by making it illegal for anyone to offer him less. We merely deprive him of the right to earn the amount that his abilities and opportunities would permit him to earn, while we deprive the community of the moderate services he is capable of rendering. In brief, for a low wage we substitute unemployment.

But I cannot devote more space to this subject here. I can only refer the reader to what I have already written on it in my *Economics in One Lesson* and *Man vs. the Welfare State,* and more especially to the careful reasoning and statistical studies of such eminent economists as professors Yale Brozen, Arthur Burns, Milton Friedman, Gottfried Haberler, and James Tobin, who have emphasized, for example, how much our continually rising legal minimum wage requirements have increased unemployment in recent years, especially among teen-aged Negroes.

Robbing Peter to Pay Paul

In the last generation there has been enacted in almost every major country of the world a whole bagful of "social" measures, most of them having the ostensible purpose of "helping

3. *Man vs. the Welfare State,* Arlington House, 1969, pp. 23–25.

the poor" in one respect or another. These include not only direct relief, but unemployment benefits, old-age benefits, sickness benefits, food subsidies, rent subsidies, farm subsidies, veterans' subsidies—in seemingly endless profusion. Many people receive not only one but many of these subsidies. The programs often overlap and duplicate each other.

What is their net effect? All of them must be paid for by that chronically forgotten man, the taxpayer. In perhaps half the cases, Paul is in effect taxed to pay for his own benefits, and gains nothing on net balance (except that he is forced to spend his earned money in other directions than he himself would have chosen). In the remaining cases, Peter is forced to pay for Paul's benefits. When any one of these schemes, or a further expansion of it, is being proposed, its political sponsors always dwell on what a generous and compassionate government should pay to Paul; they neglect to mention that this additional money must be seized from Peter. In order that Paul may receive the equivalent of more than he earns, Peter must be allowed to keep less than he earns.

The mounting burden of taxation not only undermines individual incentives to increased work and earnings, but in a score of ways discourages capital accumulation and distorts, unbalances, and shrinks production. Total real wealth and income is made smaller than it would otherwise be. On net balance there is more poverty rather than less.

But new taxes are so unpopular that most of these "social" handout schemes are originally enacted without enough increased taxation to pay for them. The result is chronic government deficits, paid for by the issuance of additional paper money. And this has led in the last quarter-century to the constant depreciation of the purchasing power of practically every currency in the world. All creditors, including the buyers of government bonds, insurance policy holders, and the depositors in savings banks, are systematically swindled. Once more the chief victims are the working and saving poor.

Yet everywhere this monetary inflation, eventually so disrup-

148

tive and ruinous to orderly balanced production, is rationalized by politicians and even by putative economists as necessary for "full employment" and "economic growth." The truth is that if this monetary inflation is persisted in, it can only lead to economic disaster.

Many of the very people who originally advocate inflation (or the policies which inevitably lead to it), when they see its consequences of raising prices and money wages, propose to cure the situation not by halting the inflation but by having the government impose price and wage controls. But all such attempts to suppress the symptoms enormously increase the harm done. Price and wage controls, to precisely the extent that they can be made temporarily effective, only distort, disrupt, and reduce production—again leading toward impoverishment.

Yet here again, as with the other false remedies for poverty referred to in this chapter, it would be an unjustifiable digression to spell out in detail all the fallacies and evil consequences of special subsidies, improvident government spending, deficit financing, monetary inflation, and price and wage controls. I have myself dealt with these subjects in two previous books: *The Failure of the New Economics*[4] and *What You Should Know About Inflation*;[5] and there is of course an extensive literature on the subject. The chief point to be reiterated here is that these policies do not help to cure poverty.

Another false remedy for poverty is the progressive income tax, as well as a very heavy burden of capital gains taxes, inheritance taxes, and corporate income taxes. All of these have the effect of discouraging production, investment, and capital accumulation. To that extent they must prolong rather than cure poverty. But these taxes have already been discussed in the chapter on dividing the wealth.

4. Princeton: Van Nostrand, 1959.
5. Princeton: Van Nostrand, 1960, 1965. Also Funk & Wagnalls paperback, 1968.

CHAPTER 15

Why Socialism Doesn't Work

WE COME NOW TO THE MOST WIDESPREAD OF ALL FALSE REMEDIES FOR poverty—outright socialism.

Now the word "socialism" is loosely used to refer to at least two distinct proposals, usually but not necessarily tied together in the minds of the proposers. One of these is the redistribution of wealth or income—if not to make incomes equal, at least to make them much more nearly equal than they are in a market economy. But the majority of those who propose this objective today think that it can be achieved by retaining the mechanism of private enterprise and then seizing part of the bigger incomes to supplement the smaller ones. This proposal has been separately considered in Chapter 11.

By "outright socialism" I refer to the Marxist proposal for "the public ownership and control of the means of production."

One of the most striking differences between the 1970s and the 1950s, or even the 1920s, is the rise in the political popularity of Socialism Two—the redistribution of income—

and the decline in the political popularity of Socialism One—government ownership and management. The reason is that the latter, in the last half-century, has been so widely tried. Particularly in Europe there is now a long history of government ownership and management of such "public utilities" as the railroads, the electric light and power industries, and the telegraph and telephone. And everywhere the history has been much the same—deficits practically always, and in the main poor service compared with what private enterprise supplied. The mail service, a government monopoly nearly everywhere, is also nearly everywhere notorious for its deficits, inefficiency, and inertia. (The contrast with the performance of "private" industry is often blurred, however, in the United States, for example, by the slow strangulation of the railroads, telephone, and power companies by government regulation and harassment.)

As a result of this history, most of the socialist parties in Europe find that they can no longer attract votes by promising to nationalize even more industries. But what is still not recognized by the socialists, by the public, or even by more than a small minority of economists, is that present government ownership and management of industries, not only in "capitalist" Europe but even in Soviet Russia, works only as well as it does because it is parasitic for accounting on the world market prices established by private enterprise.

We are so accustomed to the miracle of private enterprise that we habitually take it for granted. But how does private industry solve the incredibly complex problem of turning out tens of thousands of different goods and services in the proportions in which they are wanted by the public? How does it decide how many loaves of bread to produce and how many overcoats, how many hammers and how many houses, how many pins and how many Pontiacs, how many teaspoons and how many telephones? And how does it decide the no less difficult problem of which are the most economical and efficient methods of producing these goods?

It solves these problems through the institutions of private property, competition, the free market, and the existence of money—through the interrelations of supply and demand, costs and prices, profits and losses.

When shoes are in deficient supply compared with demand and the marginal cost of producing them, their price, and therefore the margin of profit in producing them, will increase in relation to the price and margin of profit in producing other things. Therefore the existing producers will turn out more shoes, and perhaps new producers will order machinery to make them. When the new supply catches up with existing demand, the price of shoes, and the profit in making them, will fall; the supply will no longer be increased. When hats go out of fashion and fewer are worn, the price will decline, and some may remain unsalable. Fewer hats will be made. Some producers will go out of business, and the previous labor and salvageable capital devoted to producing hats will be forced into other lines. Thus there will be a constant tendency toward equalization of profit margins (comparative risks considered) in all lines. These yearly, seasonal, or daily changes in supply and demand, cost and price, and comparative profit margins will tend to maintain a delicate but constantly changing balance in the production of the tens of thousands of different services and commodities in the proportions in which consumers demand them.

The same guide of comparative money prices and profits will also decide the kinds and proportions of capital goods that are turned out, as well as which one of hundreds of different possible methods of production is adopted in each case.

In addition, within each industry as well as between industries, competition will be taking place. Each producer will not only be trying to turn out a better product than his competitors, a product more likely to appeal to buyers, but he will be trying to reduce his cost of production as low as he possibly can in order to increase his margin of profit—or perhaps even, if his costs are already higher than average, to meet his competition and stay in business. This means that competition always tends to bring about the least-cost method of production—in other words, the most economical and efficient method of production.

Those who are most successful in this competition will acquire more capital to increase their production still further; those who are least successful will be forced out of the field. So capitalist production tends constantly to be drawn into the hands of the most efficient.

If Capitalism Did Not Exist

But how can this appallingly complex problem of supplying goods in the proportions in which consumers want them, and with the most economical production methods, be solved if the institutions of capitalism—private ownership, competition, free markets, money, prices, profits and losses—do not exist?

Suppose that all property—at least in the means of production—is taken over by the State, and that banks and money and credit are abolished as vicious capitalist institutions. How is the government to solve the problem of what goods and services to produce, of what qualities, in what proportions, in what localities, and by what technological methods?

There cannot, let us keep in mind, be a hundred or a thousand different decisions by as many different bureaucrats, with each allowed to decide independently how much of one given product must be made. The available amount of land, capital, and labor is always limited. The factors of production needed to make a given quantity of A are therefore not available for B or C; and so on. So there must be a single unified overall decision, with the relative amounts and proportions to be made of each commodity all planned in advance in relation to all the others, and with the factors of production all allocated in the corresponding proportions.

So there must be only one Master Production Plan. This could conceivably be adopted by a series of majority votes in a parliament, but in practice, to stop interminable debate and to get anything done, the broad decisions would be made by a small handful of men, and the detailed execution would probably be turned over to one Master Director who had the final word.

How would he go about solving his problem?

We must keep in mind that without free competitive markets, money, and money prices, he would be helpless. He would know, of course (if the seizure of the means of production has only recently occurred) that people under a capitalist system lived in a certain number of houses of various qualities, wore a certain amount of clothes consisting of such and such items and qualities, ate a certain amount of food consisting of such and such meats, dairy products, grains, vegetables, nuts, fruits, and beverages. The Director could simply try to continue this pre-existing mix indefinitely. But then his decisions would be completely parasitic on the previous capitalism, and he would produce and perpetuate a completely stationary or stagnant economy. If such an imitative socialism had been put into effect in, say, the France of 1870, or even of 1770, or 1670, and France had been cut off from foreign contacts, the economy of France would still be producing the same type and per capita quantity of goods and services, and by the same antiquated methods, as those that had existed in 1870, or even in 1770 or 1670, or whatever the year of socialization.

It is altogether probable that even if such a slavishly imitative production schedule were deliberately adopted, it would overlook thousands of miscellaneous small items, many of them essential, because some bureaucrat had neglected to put them into the schedule. This has happened time and again in Soviet Russia.

But let us assume that all these problems are somehow solved. How would the socialist Planners go about trying to improve on capitalist production? Suppose they decided to increase the quantity and quality of family housing. As total production is necessarily limited by existing technological knowledge and capital equipment, they could transfer land, capital, and labor to the production of more such housing only at the cost of producing less food, or less clothing, or fewer hospitals, or schools, or cars, or roads, or less of something else. How could they decide what was to be sacrificed? How would they fix the new commodity proportions?

But putting aside even this formidable problem, how would the Planners decide what machines to design, what capital goods to make, what technological methods to use, and at what localities, to produce the consumers' goods they wanted and in the proportions they wanted them?

This is not primarily a technological question, but an economic one. The purpose of economic life, the purpose of producing anything, is to increase human satisfaction, to increase human well-being. In a capitalist system, if people are not willing to pay at least as much for the consumer goods that have been produced as was paid for the labor, land, capital equipment, and raw materials that were used to produce them, it is a sign that production has been misdirected and that at least some of these productive factors have been wasted. There has been a net decrease in economic well-being instead of an increase.

There are many feasible methods—crucible, Bessemer, open-hearth, electric furnace, basic oxygen process—of making steel from iron. In fact, there are today a thousand technically feasible ways of making almost anything out of almost everything. In a private enterprise system, what decides which method will be used at a given place and time is a comparison of prospective costs.

And this necessarily means costs in terms of money. In order to compare the economic efficiency of one productive method with another, the methods must be reduced to some common denominator. Otherwise numerical comparison and calculation are impossible. In a market system this common

155

denominator is achieved by comparisons in terms of money and of prices stated in money. It is only by this means that society can determine whether a given commodity is being produced at a profit or a loss, or at what comparative profits or losses any number of different commodities are being produced.

"Playing" Free Market

In recent years even the most doctrinaire Communist countries have become aware of this. They are going to be guided hereafter, they say, by profit and loss. An industry must be profitable to justify itself. So they fix money prices for everything and measure profit and loss in monetary terms.

But this is merely "playing" free markets. This is "playing" capitalism. This imitation is the unintended flattery that the Communists now pay to the system they still ostensibly reject and denounce.

But the reason why this mock-market system has so far proved so disappointing is that the Communist governments do not know how to fix prices. They have achieved whatever success they have had when they have simply used the quotations they found already existing for international commodities in the speculative markets—i.e., in the capitalist markets—in the Western world. But there are a limited number of such grains and raw materials with international markets. In any case, their prices change daily, and are always for specific grades at specific locations.

In trying to fix prices for commodities and for the multitudinous objects not quoted on these international markets the Communist countries are at sea. The Marxist labor theory of value is false and therefore useless to them. We cannot measure the value of anything by the number of hours of "labor time" put into it. There are, for one thing, enormous differences in the skill, quality, and productivity of different people's labor.

Nor can we, as suggested by some Soviet economists, base prices on "actual costs of production." Costs of production are themselves prices—the prices of raw materials, of factories and machinery, rent, interest, the wages of labor, and so on.

And nowhere, in a free market, are prices for long exactly equal to costs of production. It is precisely the *differences* between prices and costs of production that are constantly, in a free market economy, redirecting and changing the balance of production as among thousands of different commodities and services. In industries where market prices are well above existing marginal costs of production, there will be a great incentive to increase output, as well as increased means to do it. In industries where prices fall below marginal costs of production, output must shrink. Everywhere supply will keep adjusting itself to demand.

Where prices have been set arbitrarily, real profits and losses cannot be determined. If I am a commissar in charge of an automobile factory, and do not own the money I pay out, and you are a commissar in charge of a steel plant, and do not own the steel you sell or retain for yourself the money you sell it for, and we are each ordered to show a profit, the first thing each of us will do is to appeal to the Central Planning Board to set an advantageous price (to him) for steel and for automobiles. As an automobile commissar, I will want the price of the cars I sell to be set as high as possible, and the price of the steel I buy to be set as low as possible, so that my own "profit" record will look good or my bonus will be fixed high. But as a steel commissar, you will want the selling price of your steel to be fixed as high as possible, and your own cost prices to be fixed low, for the same reason. But when prices are thus fixed blindly, politically, and arbitrarily, who will know what any industry's real profits or losses (as distinguished from its nominal bookkeeping profits or losses) have been?

The problems of centralized direction of an economy are so insuperable that in socialist countries there are periodically experiments in decentralization. But in an economy only half free—that is, in an economy in which every factory is free to decide how much to produce of what, but in which the basic prices, wages, rents, and interest rates are blindly fixed or guessed at by the sole ultimate owner of the means of production, the State—a decentralized system could quickly become even more chaotic than a centralized one. If finished products *m, n, o, p,* and so on are made from raw materials *a, b, c, d,* and so on, in various combinations and proportions, how can the individual producers of the raw materials know how much of each to produce, and at what rate, unless they know how much the producers of the finished products plan to produce of the latter, how much raw materials the latter are going to need, and just *when* they are going to need them? And how can the individual producer of raw material *a* or of finished product *m* know how much of it to produce unless he knows how much of that raw material or finished product others in his line are planning to produce, as well as relatively how much ultimate consumers are going to want or demand?

An economic system without private property and free-market price guides must be chaotic. In a Communistic system, centralized or decentralized, there will always be unbalanced and unmatched production, shortages of this and unusable surpluses of that, duplications, bottlenecks, time lags, inefficiency, and appalling waste.

In brief, socialism is incapable of solving the incredibly complicated problem of economic calculation. That problem can be solved only by capitalism.[6]

6. For a fuller discussion of the problem of economic calculation, see the present writer's novel *Time Will Run Back* (originally published by Appleton-Century-Crofts in 1951 as *The Great Idea,* and republished under the new title by Arlington House in 1966). And see especially the discussion by the great seminal thinker who has done more than any other to make other economists aware of the existence, nature, and extent of the problem, Ludwig von Mises, in his *Socialism: An Analysis,* London: Jonathan Cape, 1936, 1951, 1953, 1969, and in his *Human Action* (Chicago: Henry Regnery, 3rd. rev. ed., 1963, pp. 200–231 and 698–715. See also *Collectivist Economic Planning,* edited by F. A. Hayek, London: George Routledge, 1935, and *Economic Calculation in the Socialist Society,* by T. J. B. Hoff, London: William Hodge, 1949.

CHAPTER 16

Foreign Investment vs. "Aid"

AT THE BEGINNING OF CHAPTER III OF HIS *History of England,* Thomas Babington Macaulay wrote:

"In every experimental science there is a tendency toward perfection. In every human being there is a wish to ameliorate his own condition. These two principles have often sufficed, even when counteracted by great public calamities and by bad institutions, to carry civilization rapidly forward. No ordinary misfortune, no ordinary misgovernment, will do so much to make a nation wretched as the constant effort of every man to better himself will do to make a nation prosperous. It has often been found that profuse expenditures, heavy taxation, absurd commercial restrictions, corrupt tribunals, disastrous wars, seditions, persecutions, conflagrations, inundations, have not been able to destroy capital so fast as the exertions of private citizens have been able to create it. It can easily be proved that, in our own land, the national wealth has, during at least six centuries, been almost uninterruptedly increasing. . . . This progress, having continued during many ages, became at length, about the middle of the eighteenth century, portentously rapid, and has proceeded, during the nineteenth, with accelerated velocity."

We too often forget this basic truth. Would-be humanitarians speak constantly today of "the vicious circle of poverty." Poverty, they tell us, produces malnutrition and disease, which produce apathy and idleness, which perpetuate poverty; and no progress is possible without help from outside. This theory is today propounded unceasingly, as if it were axiomatic. Yet the history of nations and individuals shows it to be false.

It is not only "the natural effort which every man is continually making to better his own condition" (as Adam Smith put it even before Macaulay) that we need to consider, but the constant effort of most families to give their children a "better start" than they enjoyed themselves. The poorest people under the most primitive conditions work first of all for food, then for clothing and shelter. Once they have provided a rudimentary shelter, more of their energies are released for increasing the quantity or improving the quality of their food and clothing and shelter. And for providing tools. Once they have acquired a few tools, part of their time and energies can be released for making more and better tools. And so, as Macaulay emphasized, economic progress can become accelerative.

One reason it took so many centuries before this acceleration actually began is that as men increased their production of the means of subsistence more of their children survived. This meant that their increased production was in fact mainly used to support an increasing population. Aggregate production, population, and consumption all increased; but per capita production and consumption barely increased at all. Not until the Industrial Revolution began in the late eighteenth century did the rate of production begin to increase by so much that, in spite of leading to an unprecedented increase in population, it led also to an increase in per capita production. In the Western world this increase has continued ever since.

160

So a country can, in fact, starting from the most primitive conditions, lift itself from poverty to abundance. If this were not so, the world could never have arrived at its present state of wealth. Every country started poor. As a matter of historic fact, most nations raised themselves from "hopeless" poverty to at least a less wretched poverty purely by their own efforts.

One of the ways by which each nation or region did this was by division of labor within its own territory and by the mutual exchange of services and products. Each man enormously increased his output by eventually specializing in a single activity—by becoming a farmer, butcher, baker, mason, bricklayer, or tailor—and exchanging his product with his neighbors. In time this process extended beyond national boundaries, enabling each nation to specialize more than before in the products or services that it was able to supply more plentifully or cheaply than others, and by exchange and trade to supply itself with goods and services from others more plentifully or cheaply than it could supply them for itself.

But this was only one way in which foreign trade accelerated the mutual enrichment of nations. In addition to being able to supply itself with more goods and cheaper goods as a result of foreign trade, each nation supplied itself with goods and services that it could otherwise not produce at all, and of which it would perhaps not even have known the existence.

Thus foreign trade *educates* each nation that participates in it, and not only through such obvious means as the exchange of books and periodicals. This educational effect is particularly important when hitherto backward countries open their doors to industrially advanced countries. One of the most dramatic examples of this occurred in 1854, when Commodore Perry at the head of a U.S. naval force "persuaded" the Japanese, after 250 years of isolation, to open their doors to trade and communication with the United States and the rest of the world.

Part of Perry's success, significantly, was the result of bringing and showing the Japanese such things as a modern telescope, a model telegraph and a model railway, which delighted and amazed them.

Western reformers today, praising some hitherto backward country in Africa or Asia, will explain how much smarter its natives are than we of the West because they have "jumped in a single decade from the seventeenth into the twentieth century." But the jump, while praiseworthy, is not so surprising when one recalls that what the natives mainly did was to import the machines, technology, and know-how that had been developed during those three centuries by the scientists and technicians of the West. The backward countries were able to bypass home coal furnaces, gaslight, the street car and even, in some cases, the railroad, and to import Western automobiles, Western knowledge of road-building, Western airplanes and airliners, telephones, central oil heaters, electric light, radio and television, refrigerators and air-conditioning, electric heaters, stoves, dishwashers and clothes washers, machine tools, factories, plants, and Western technicians, and then to send some of their youth to Western colleges and universities to become technicians, engineers, and scientists. The backward countries imported, in brief, their "great leap forward."

In fact, not merely the recently backward countries of Asia and Africa, but every great industrialized Western nation, not excluding the United States, owes a very great part—indeed, the major part—of its present technological knowledge and productivity to discoveries, inventions, and improvements imported from other nations. Notwithstanding the elegant elucidations by the classical economists, very few of us today appreciate all that the world and each nation owes to foreign trade, not only in services and products, but even more in knowledge, ideas, and ideals.

Trade Leads to Investment

Historically, international trade gradually led to international investment. Among independent nations, international investment developed inevitably when the exporters of one nation, in order to increase their sales, sold on short-term credit, and later on longer-term credit, to the importers of another. It developed also because capital was scarcer in the less developed nation, and interest rates were higher. It developed on a larger scale when men emigrated from one country to another, starting businesses in the new country, taking their capital as well as their skills with them.

In fact, what is now known as "portfolio" investment—the purchase by the nationals of one country of the stocks or bonds of the companies of another—has usually been less important quantitatively than this "direct" investment. In 1967 U.S. private investments abroad were estimated to total $93 billion, of which $12 billion were short-term assets and claims, and $81 billion long-term. Of American long-term private investments abroad $22 billion were portfolio investments and $59 billion direct investments.

The export of private capital for private investment has on the whole been extremely profitable for the capital-exporting countries. In every one of the twenty years from 1945 to 1964 inclusive, for example, the income from old direct foreign investments by U.S. companies exceeded the outflow of new direct investments. In that twenty-year period new outflows of direct investments totaled $22.8 billion, but income from old direct investments came to $37.1 billion, plus $4.6 billion from royalties and fees, leaving an excess inflow of $18.9 billion. In fact, with the exception of 1928, 1929 and 1931, U.S. income from direct foreign investments exceeded new capital outlays in every year since 1919.[1]

1. See *The United States Balance of Payments,* Washington: International Economic Policy Association, 1966, pp. 21 and 22.

Our direct foreign investments also greatly stimulated our merchandise exports. The U.S. Department of Commerce found that in 1964, for example, $6.3 billion, or 25 percent of our total exports in that year, went to affiliates of American companies overseas.

It is one of the ironies of our time, however, that the U.S. Government decided to put the entire blame for the recent "balance-of-payments deficit" on American investments abroad; and beginning in mid-1963, started to penalize and restrict such investment.

The advantages of international investment to the capital importing country should be even more obvious. In any backward country there are almost unlimited potential ventures, or "investment opportunities," that are not undertaken chiefly because the capital to start them does not exist. It is the domestic lack of capital that makes it so difficult for the "underdeveloped" country to climb out of its wretched condition. Outside capital can enormously accelerate its rate of improvement.

Investment from abroad, like domestic investment, can be of two kinds: the first is in the form of fixed interest-bearing loans, the second in the form of direct equity investment in which the foreign investor takes both the risks and the profits. The politicians of the capital-importing country usually prefer the first. They see their nationals, say, making 15 or 30 percent annual gross profit on a venture, paying off the foreign lender at a rate of only 6 percent, and keeping the difference as net profit. If the foreign investor makes a similar assessment of the situation, however, he naturally prefers to make the direct equity investment himself.

But the foreigner's preference in this regard does not necessarily mean that the capital-importing country is injured. It is to its own advantage if its government puts no vexatious restrictions on the form or conditions of the private foreign investment. For if the foreign investor imports, in addition to his capital, his own (usually) superior management, experience, and technical know-how, his enterprise may be more likely to succeed. He cannot help but give employment to labor in the capital-importing country, even if he is allowed to bring in labor freely from his own. Self-interest and wage-rate differentials will probably soon lead him to displace most of whatever common or even skilled labor he originally brings in from his own country with the labor of the host country. He will usually supply the capital-importing country itself with some article or amenity it did not have before. He will raise the average marginal productivity of labor in the country in which he has built his plant or made his investment, and his enterprise will tend to raise wages there. And if his investment proves particularly profitable, he will probably keep reinvesting most of his profits in it as long as the market seems to justify the reinvestment.

There is still another benefit to the capital-importing country from private foreign investment. The foreign investors will naturally seek out first the most profitable investment opportunities. If they choose wisely, these will also be the investments that produce the greatest surplus of market value over costs and are therefore economically most productive. When the originally most productive investment opportunities have been exploited to a point where the comparative rate of return begins to diminish, the foreign investors will look for the next most productive investment opportunities, originally passed over. And so on. Private foreign investment will therefore tend to promote the most rapid rate of economic growth.

Both Sides Gain

It is unfortunate, however, that just as the government of the private-capital-exporting country today tends to regard its capital exports with alarm as a threat to its "balance of payments," the government of the private-capital-importing country today tends to regard its capital imports at least with suspicion if not with even greater alarm. Doesn't the private-capital-exporting country make a profit on this capital? And if so, mustn't this profit necessarily be at the expense of the capital-importing country? Mustn't the latter country somehow be giving away its patrimony? It seems impossible for the anticapitalist mentality (which prevails among the politicians of the world, particularly in the underdeveloped countries) to recognize that both sides normally benefit from any voluntary economic transaction, whether a purchase-sale or a loan-investment, domestic or international.

Chief among the many fears of the politicians of the capital-importing country is that foreign investors "take the money out of the country." To the extent that this is true, it is true also of domestic investment. If a home owner in Philadelphia gets a mortgage from an investor in New York, he may point out that his interest and amortization payments are going out of Philadelphia and even out of Pennsylvania. But he can do this with a straight face only by forgetting that he originally borrowed the money from the New York lender either because he could not raise it at all in his home city or because he got better terms than he could get in his home city. If the New Yorker makes an equity investment in Pennsylvania, he may take out all the net profits; but he probably employs Pennsylvania labor to build his factory and operate it. And he probably pays out $85 to $90 annually for labor, supplies, rent, etc., mainly in Pennsylvania, for every $10 he takes back to New York. (In 1970, American manufacturing corporations showed a net profit after Federal income taxes of only 4 cents per dollar of sales.) "They take the money out of the country" is an objection against foreign investors resulting even more from xenophobia than from anticapitalism.

Another objection to foreign investment by politicians of the capital-importing country is that the foreign investors may "dominate" the borrowing country's economy. The implication (made in 1965 by the de Gaulle government of France, for example) is that American-owned companies might come to have

166

too much to say about the economic decisions of the government of the countries in which they are located. The real danger, however, is the other way round. The foreign-owned company puts itself at the mercy of the government of the host country. Its capital, in the form of buildings, equipment, drilled wells and refineries, developed mines, and even bank deposits, may be trapped. In the last twenty-five years, particularly in Latin America and the Middle East, as American oil companies and others have found to their sorrow, the dangers of discriminatory labor legislation, onerous taxation, harassment, or even expropriation are very real.

Yet the anticapitalist, xenophobic, and other prejudices against private foreign investment have been so widespread, in both the countries that would gain from importing capital and the countries that would profit from exporting it, that the governments in both sets of countries have imposed taxes, laws and regulations, red tape, and other obstacles to discourage it.

At the same time, paradoxically, there has grown up in the last quarter-century powerful political pressures in both sets of countries in favor of the richer countries *giving capital away* to the poorer in the form of government-to-government "aid."

Origin of Marshall Plan

This present curious giveaway mania (it can only be called that on the part of the countries making the grants) got started as the result of an historical accident. During World War II, the United States had been pouring supplies—munitions, industrial equipment, foodstuffs—into the countries of its allies and co-belligerents. These were all nominally "loans." To cite the two outstanding cases, American Lend-Lease to Great Britain came to some $30 billion and to Soviet Russia to $11 billion.

But when the war ended, Americans were informed not only that the Lend-Lease recipients could not repay and had no intention of repaying, but that the countries receiving these loans in war time had become dependent upon them and were still in desperate straits, and that further credits were necessary to stave off disaster.

This was the origin of the Marshall Plan.

On June 5, 1947, General George C. Marshall, then American Secretary of State, delivered at Harvard the world's most expensive commencement address. He said:

"The truth of the matter is that Europe's requirements, for the next three or four years, of foreign food and other essential products—principally from America—are so much greater than her present ability to pay that she must have substantial additional help, or face economic, social and political deterioration of a very grave character."

Whereupon Congress authorized the spending in the following three-and-a-half years of some $12 billion in aid.

This aid was widely credited with restoring economic health to "free" Europe and halting the march of Communism in the recipient countries. It is true that Europe did finally recover from the ravages of World War II—as it had recovered from the ravages of World War I. And it is true that, apart from Yugoslavia, the countries not occupied by Soviet Russia did not go Communist. But whether the Marshall Plan accelerated or retarded this recovery, or substantially affected the extent of Communist penetration in Europe, can never be proved. What can be said is that the plight of Europe in 1947 was at least as much the result of misguided European governmental economic policies as of physical devastation caused by the war. Europe's recovery was far slower than it could have been, with or without the Marshall plan.

The German "Miracle"

This was dramatically demonstrated in West Germany in 1948, when the actions between June 20 and July 8 of Economic Minister Ludwig Erhard in simultaneously halting inflation, introducing a thoroughgoing currency reform, and removing the strangling network of price controls brought the German "miracle" of recovery.

As Dr. Erhard himself described his action: "We decided upon and reintroduced the old rules of a free economy, the rules of *laissez-faire.* We abolished practically all controls over allocation, prices and wages and replaced them with a price mechanism controlled predominamtly by money."

The result was that German industrial production in the second half of 1948 rose from 45 percent to nearly 75 percent of the 1936 level, while steel production doubled that year.

It is sometimes claimed that it was Germany's share of Marshall aid that brought on the recovery. But nothing similar occurred in Great Britain, for example, which received more than twice as much Marshall aid. The German per capita gross national product, measured in constant prices, increased 64 percent between 1950 and 1958, whereas the per capita increase in Great Britain, similarly measured, rose only 15 percent.

Once American politicians got the idea that the American taxpayer owed other countries a living, it followed logically that his duty could not be limited to just a few. Surely that duty was to see that poverty was abolished everywhere in the world. And so in his inaugural address of January 20, 1949, President Truman called for "a bold new program" to make "the benefits of our scientific advances and industrial progress available for the improvement and growth of underdeveloped areas. . . .This program can greatly increase the industrial activity in other nations and can raise substantially their standards of living."

Because it was so labeled in the Truman address, this program became known as "Point Four." Under it the "emergency" foreign aid of the Marshall Plan, which was originally to run for three or four years at most, was universalized, and has now been running for more than twenty years. So far as its advocates and built-in bureaucracy are concerned, it is to last until foreign poverty has been abolished from the face of the earth, or until the per capita "gap" between incomes in the backward countries and the advanced countries has been closed—even if that takes forever.

The cost of the program has already been appalling. Total disbursements to foreign nations, in the fiscal years 1946 through 1971, came to $138 billion. The total net interest paid on what the United States borrowed to give away these funds amounted in the same period to $74 billion, bringing the grand total through the 26-year period to $213 billion.[2]

This money went altogether to some 130 nations. Even in the fiscal year 1972, the aid program was still operating in 98 nations of the world, with 55,000 persons on the payroll, including U.S. and foreign personnel. Congressman Otto E. Passman, chairman of the Foreign Operations Subcommittee on Appropriations, declared on July 1, 1971: "Of the three-and-a-half billion people of the world, all but 36 million have received aid from the U.S."

Even the colossal totals just cited do not measure the total loss that the foreign giveaway program has imposed on the American economy. Foreign aid has had the most serious economic side effects. It has led to grave distortions in our economy. It has undermined our currency, and contributed toward driving us off the gold standard. It has accelerated our inflation. It was sufficient in itself to account for the total of our Federal deficits in the 1946–72 period. The $213-billion foreign aid total exceeds by $73 billion even the $140-billion increase in our gross national debt during the same years. Foreign aid was also sufficient in itself to account for all our balance-of-payments deficits up to 1970 (which our government's policies blamed on private foreign investment).

The advocates of foreign aid may choose to argue that though our chronic Federal budget deficits in the last 26 years *could* be

2. Source: Foreign Operations Subcommittee on Appropriations, House of Representatives, July 1, 1970.

imputed to foreign aid, we could alternately impute those deficits to other expenditures, and assume that the foreign aid was paid for entirely by raising additional taxes. But such an assumption would hardly improve the case for foreign aid. It would mean that taxes during this quarter-century averaged at least $5 billion higher each year than they would have otherwise. It would be difficult to exaggerate the setbacks to personal working incentives, to new ventures, to profits, to capital investment, to employment, to wages, to living standards, that an annual burden of $5 billion in additional taxation can cause.

If, finally, we make the "neutral" assumption that our $138 or $213 billion in foreign aid (whichever way we choose to calculate the sum) was financed in exact proportion to our actual deficit and tax totals in the 26-year period, we merely make it responsible for part of both sets of evils.

Foreign Aid Set Us Back

In sum, the foreign aid program has immensely set back our own potential capital development. It ought to be obvious that a foreign giveaway program can raise the standards of living of the so-called "underdeveloped areas" of the world only by lowering our own living standards compared with what they could otherwise be. If our taxpayers are forced to contribute millions of dollars for hydroelectric plants in Africa or Asia, they obviously have that much less for productive investment in the United States. If they contribute $10 million dollars for a housing project in Uruguay, they have just that much less for their own housing, or any other cost equivalent, at home. Even our own socialist and statist do-gooders would be shaken if it occurred to them to consider how much might have been done with that $138 or $213 billion of foreign aid to mitigate pollution at home, build subsidized housing, and relieve "the plight of our cities." Free enterprisers, of course, will lament the foreign giveaway on the far more realistic calculation of how enormously the production, and the wealth and welfare of every class of our population, could have been increased by $138 to $213 billion in more private investment in new and better tools and cost-reducing equipment, in higher living standards, and in more and better homes, hospitals, schools and universities.

What have been the economic or political compensations to the United States for the staggering cost of its foreign aid program? Most of them have been illusory.

When our successive Presidents and foreign aid officials make inspirational speeches in favor of foreign aid, they dwell chiefly on its alleged humanitarian virtues, on the need for American generosity and compassion, on our duty to relieve the suffering and share the burdens of all mankind. But when they are trying to get the necessary appropriations out of Congress, they recognize the advisability of additional arguments. So they appeal to the American taxpayer's material self-interest. It will redound to his benefit, they argue, in three ways: 1. It will increase our foreign trade, and consequently the profits from it. 2. It will keep the underdeveloped countries from going Communist. 3. It will turn the recipients of our grants into our eternally grateful friends.

The answers to these arguments are clear:

1. Particular exporters may profit on net balance from the foreign aid program, but they necessarily do so at the expense of the American taxpayer. It makes little difference in the end whether we give other countries the dollars to pay for our goods, or whether we directly give them the goods. We cannot grow rich by giving our goods or our dollars away. We can only grow poorer. (I would be ashamed of stating this truism if our foreign aid advocates did not so systematically ignore it.)

2. There is no convincing evidence that our foreign aid played any role whatever in reversing, halting, or even slowing down any drift toward Communism. Our aid to Cuba in the early years of the program, and even our special favoritism

172

toward it in assigning sugar quotas and the like, did not prevent it from going Communist in 1958. Our $760 million of aid to the United Arab Republic did not prevent it from coming under Russian domination. Our $465 million aid to Peru did not prevent it from seizing American private properties there; nor did our $1,282 million aid to Chile. Neither our $8,004 million aid to India, nor our $4,484 million aid to Pakistan, prevented either country from moving deeper and deeper into socialism and despotic economic controls. Our aid, in fact, subsidized these very programs, or made them possible.

And so it goes, country after country.

3. Instead of turning the recipients into grateful friends, there is ever-fresh evidence that our foreign aid program has had precisely the opposite effect. It is pre-eminently the American embassies and the official American libraries that are mobbed and stoned, the American flag that is burned, the Yanks that are told to go home. And the head of almost every government that accepts American aid finds it necessary to denounce and insult the United States at regular intervals in order to prove to his own people that he is not subservient and no puppet.

So foreign aid hurts both the economic and political interest of the country that extends it.

How Aid Hurts the Receiver

But all this might be overlooked, in a broad humanitarian view, if foreign aid accomplished its main ostensible purpose of raising the living levels of the countries that received it. Yet both reason and experience make it clear that in the long run it has precisely the opposite effect.

Of course a country cannot give away $138 billion without its doing *something* abroad. (Though we must always keep in mind the reservation—instead of something *else* at home.) If the money is spent on a public housing project, on a hydroelectric dam, on a steel mill (no matter how uneconomic or ill-advised), the housing or the dam or the mill is brought into existence. It is visible and undeniable. But to point to that is to point only to the visible gross gain while ignoring the costs and the offsets. In all sorts of ways—economic, political, spiritual— the aid in the long run hurts the recipient country. It becomes dependent on the aid. It loses self-respect and self-reliance. The poor country becomes a pauperized country, a beggar country.

There is a profound contrast between the effects of foreign aid and of voluntary private investment. Foreign aid goes from government to government. It is therefore almost inevitably statist and socialistic. A good part of it goes into providing more goods for immediate consumption, which may do nothing to increase the country's productive capacity. The rest goes into government projects, government Five-Year Plans, govern- ment airlines, government hydroelectric plants and dams, or government steel mills, erected principally for prestige rea- sons, and for looking impressive in colored photographs, and regardless of whether the projects are economically justified or self-supporting. As a result, real economic growth is retarded.

From the very beginning, foreign aid has faced an insoluble dilemma. I called attention to this in a book published in 1947, *Will Dollars Save the World?,* when the Marshall Plan was proposed but not yet enacted:

"Inter-governmental loans [they have since become mainly gifts, which only intensifies the problem] are on the horns of this dilemma. If on the one hand they are made without condi- tions, the funds are squandered and dissipated and fail to ac- complish their purpose. They may even be used for the precise opposite of the purpose that the lender had in mind. But if the lending government attempts to impose conditions, its attempt causes immediate resentment. It is called 'dollar diplomacy,' or 'American imperialism,' or 'interfering in the internal affairs' of the borrowing nation. The resentment is quickly exploited by the Communists in that nation."

In the 26 years since the foreign-aid program was launched, the administrators have not only failed to find their way out of this dilemma; they have refused even to acknowledge its existence. They have zigzagged from one course to the other, and ended by following the worst course of all: they have insisted that the recipient governments adopt "growth policies"— which mean, in practice, government "planning," controls, inflation, ambitious nationalized projects—in brief, socialism.

If the foreign aid were not offered in the first place, the recipient government would find it advisable to try to attract foreign private investment. To do this it would have to abandon its socialistic and inflationary policies, its exchange controls, its laws against taking money out of the country. It would have to abandon harassment of private business, restrictive labor laws, and discriminatory taxation. It would have to give assurances against nationalization, expropriation, and seizure.

Specifically, if the nationals of a poor country wanted to borrow foreign capital for a private project, and had to pay a going rate of, say, 7 percent interest for the loan, their project would have to be one that promised to yield at least 7 percent before the foreign investors would be interested. If the government of the poor country, on the other hand, can get the money from a foreign government without having to pay interest at all, it need not trouble to ask itself whether the proposed project is likely to prove economic and self-liquidating or not. The essential market guide to comparative need and utility is then completely removed. What decides priorities is the grandiose dreams of the government planners, unembarrassed by bothersome calculations of comparative costs and usefulness.

Where foreign government aid is not freely offered, however, a poor country, to attract private foreign investment, must establish an actual record of respecting private property and maintaining free markets. Such a free-enterprise policy by itself, even if it did not at first attract a single dollar of foreign investment, would give enormous stimulus to the economy of

175

the country that adopted it. It would first of all stop the flight of capital on the part of its own nationals and stimulate *domestic* investment. It is constantly forgotten that both domestic and foreign capital investment are encouraged (or discouraged) by the same means.

It is not true, to repeat, that the poor countries are necessarily caught in a "vicious circle of poverty," from which they cannot escape without massive handouts from abroad. It is not true that "the rich countries are getting richer while the poor countries are getting poorer." It is not true that the "gap" between the living standards of the poor countries and the rich countries is growing ever wider. Certainly that is not true in any *proportionate* sense. From 1945 to 1955, for example, the average rate of growth of Latin American countries in national income was 4.5 percent per annum, and in output per head 2.4 percent—both rates appreciably higher than the corresponding figure for the United States.[3]

The foreign aid ideology is merely the relief ideology, the guaranteed-income ideology, applied on an international scale. Its remedy, like the domestic relief remedy, is to "abolish poverty" by seizing from the rich to give to the poor. Both proposals systematically ignore the reasons for the poverty they seek to cure. Neither draws any distinction between the poverty caused by misfortune and the poverty brought on by shiftlessness and folly. The advocates of both proposals forget that their chief attention should be directed to restoring the incentives, self-reliance, and *production* of the poor family or the poor

3. Cf. "Some observations on 'Gapology,'" by P. T. Bauer and John B. Wood in *Economic Age* (London), November-December, 1969. Professor Bauer is one of the few academic economists who have seriously analyzed the fallacies of foreign aid. See also his Yale lecture on foreign aid published by The Institute of Economic Affairs (London), 1966, and his article on "Development Economics" in *Roads to Freedom: Essays in Honour of Friedrich A. von Hayek* (London: Routledge & Kegan Paul, 1969). I may also refer the reader to my own book *Will Dollars Save the World?*, Appleton, 1947, to my pamphlet *Illusions of Point Four,* Irvington-on-Hudson, New York: Foundation for Economic Education, 1950, and to the chapter on "The Fallacy of Foreign Aid" in my *Man vs. the Welfare State,* Arlington House, 1969.

country, and that the principal means of doing this is through the free market.

In sum, government-to-government foreign aid promotes statism, *dirigisme,* socialism, dependence, pauperization, inefficiency and waste. It prolongs the poverty it is designed to cure. Voluntary private investment in private enterprise, on the other hand, promotes capitalism, production, independence and self-reliance. It is by attracting foreign private investment that the great industrial nations of the world were once helped. It is so that America itself was helped by British capital, in the latter half of the nineteenth century, in building its railroads and exploiting its great national resources. It is so that the still "underdeveloped areas" of the world can most effectively be helped today to develop their own great potentialities and to raise the living standards of their masses.

CHAPTER 17

Why Some Are Poorer

THROUGHOUT HISTORY, UNTIL ABOUT THE MIDDLE OF THE EIGHTEENTH century, mass poverty was nearly everywhere the normal condition of man. Then capital accumulation and a series of major inventions ushered in the Industrial Revolution. In spite of occasional setbacks, economic progress became accelerative. Today, in the United States, in Canada, in nearly all of Europe, in Australia, New Zealand, and Japan, mass poverty has been practically eliminated. It has either been conquered or is in process of being conquered by a progressive capitalism. Mass poverty is still found in most of Latin America, most of Asia, and most of Africa.

Yet even the United States, the most affluent of all countries, continues to be plagued by "pockets" of poverty and by individual poverty.

Temporary pockets of poverty, or of distress, can be sometimes incident to a free competitive enterprise system. In such a system some firms and industries are growing or being born, others are shrinking or dying; and many entrepreneurs and workers in the dying industries are unwilling or unable to change their residence or their occupation. Pockets of poverty may be the result of a failure to meet domestic or foreign competition, of a shrinkage or disappearance of demand for some product, of mines or wells that have been exhausted, or land that has become a dust bowl, and of droughts, blights, earthquakes, and other natural disasters. There is no way of preventing most of these contingencies, and no all-encompassing cure for them. Each is likely to call for its own special measures of alleviation or adjustment. Whatever general measures may be advisable can best be considered as part of the broader problem of individual poverty.

This problem is nearly always referred to by socialists as "the paradox of poverty in the midst of plenty." The implication of the phrase is not only that such poverty is inexcusable, but that its existence must be the fault of those who have the "plenty." We are most likely to see the problem clearly, however, if we stop blaming "society" in advance and seek an unemotional analysis.

When we start seriously to itemize the causes of individual poverty, absolute or relative, they seem too diverse and numerous even to classify. Yet in most discussion we do find the causes of individual poverty tacitly divided into two distinct groups—those that are the fault of the poor themselves and those that are not. Historically, many so-called "conservatives" have tended to blame poverty entirely on the poor: they are shiftless, or drunks or bums: "Let them go to work." Most so-called "liberals," on the other hand, have tended to blame poverty on everybody but the poor: they are at worst the "unfortunate," the "underprivileged," if not actually the "exploited," the "victims" of the "maldistribution of wealth," or of "heartless *laissez faire.*"

The truth, of course, is not that simple, either way. We may, occasionally, come upon an individual who seems to be poor through no fault whatever of his own (or rich through no merit of his own). And we may occasionally find one who seems to be poor entirely through his own fault (or rich entirely through his own merit.) But most often we find an inextricable mixture of causes for any given person's relative poverty or wealth. And any quantitative estimate of fault versus misfortune seems purely arbitrary. Are we entitled to say, for example, that any given individual's poverty is only 1 percent his own fault, or 99 percent his own fault—or fix any definite percentage whatever? Can we make any reasonably accurate quantitative estimate of the percentage even of those who are poor *mainly* through their own fault, as compared with those whose poverty is mainly the result of circumstances beyond their control? Do we, in fact, have any *objective* standards for making the separation?

Fixing the Blame

A good idea of some of the older ways of approaching the problem can be obtained from the article "Poverty" in *The Encyclopedia of Social Reform*, published in 1897.[1] This refers to a table compiled by a Professor A. G. Warner in his book *American Charities*. This table brought together the results of investigations in 1890 to 1892 by the charity organization societies of Baltimore, Buffalo, and New York City; the associated charities of Boston and Cincinnati; the studies of Charles Booth in Stepney and St. Pancras parishes in London; and the statements of Böhmert for seventy-six German cities published in 1886. Each of these studies tried to determine the "chief cause" of poverty for each of the paupers or poor families it listed. Twenty such "chief causes" were listed altogether.

Professor Warner converted the number of cases listed under each cause in each study into percentages, wherever this had not already been done; then took an unweighted average of the

1. William D. P. Bliss, ed., New York: Funk & Wagnalls.

results obtained in the fifteen studies for each of these "Causes of Poverty as Determined by Case Counting," and came up with the following percentages. First came six "Causes Indicating Misconduct": Drink, 11.0 percent; Immorality, 4.7; Laziness, 6.2; Inefficiency and Shiftlessness, 7.4; Crime and Dishonesty, 1.2; and Roving Disposition, 2.2—making a total of causes due to misconduct of 32.7 percent.

Professor Warner next itemized fourteen "Causes Indicating Misfortune": Imprisonment of Bread Winner, 1.5 percent; Orphans and Abandoned, 1.4; Neglect by Relatives, 1.0; No Male Support, 8.0; Lack of Employment, 17.4; Insufficient Employment, 6.7; Poorly Paid Employment, 4.4; Unhealthy or Dangerous Employment, 0.4; Ignorance of English, 0.6; Accident, 3.5; Sickness or Death in Family, 23.6; Physical Defect, 4.1; Insanity, 1.2; and Old Age, 9.6—making a total of causes indicating misfortune of 84.4 percent.

Let me say at once that as a statistical exercise this table is close to worthless, full of more confusions and discrepancies than it seems worth analyzing here. Weighted and unweighted averages are hopelessly mixed. Certainly it seems strange, for example, to list all cases of unemployment under "misfortune" and none under personal shortcomings.

Even Professor Warner points out how arbitrary most of the figures are: "A man has been shiftless all his life, and is now old; is the cause of poverty shiftlessness or old age? . . . Perhaps there is hardly a single case in the whole 7,000 where destitution has resulted from a single cause."

But though the table has little value as an effort in quantification, any attempt to name and classify the causes of poverty does call attention to how many and varied such causes there can be, and to the difficulty of separating those that are an individual's own fault from those that are not.

An effort to apply objective standards is now made by the Social Security Administration and other Federal agencies by classifying poor families under "conditions associated with poverty." Thus we get comparative tabulations of incomes of farm and nonfarm families, of white and Negro families, families classified by age of "head," male head or female head, size of family, number of members under eighteen, educational attainment of head (years in elementary schools, high school, or college), employment status of head, work experience of head (how many weeks worked or idle), "main reason for not working: ill or disabled, keeping house, going to school, unable to find work, other, 65 years and over"; occupation of longest job of head, number of earners in family; and so on.

These classifications, and their relative numbers and comparative incomes, do throw objective light on the problem, but much still depends on how the results are interpreted.

Living from Moment to Moment

A provocative thesis has been put forward by Professor Edward C. Banfield of Harvard.[2] He divides American society into four "class cultures": upper, middle, working, and lower classes. These "subcultures," he warns, are not necessarily determined by present economic status, but by the distinctive psychological orientation of each toward providing for a more or less distant future.

At the most future-oriented end of this scale, the upper-class individual expects long life, looks forward to the future of his children, grandchildren, even great-grandchildren, and is concerned also for the future of such abstract entities as the community, nation, or mankind. He is confident that within rather wide limits he can, if he exerts himself to do so, shape the future to accord with his purposes. He therefore has strong incentives to "invest" in the improvement of the future situation—i.e., to sacrifice some present satisfaction in the expectation of enabling someone (himself, his children, mankind, etc.)

2. Edward C. Banfield, *The Unheavenly City*, Boston: Little, Brown, 1970.

182

to enjoy greater satisfactions at some future time. As contrasted with this:

"The lower-class individual lives from moment to moment. If he has any awareness of a future, it is of something fixed, fated, beyond his control: things happen *to* him, he does not *make* them happen. Impulse governs his behavior, either because he cannot discipline himself to sacrifice a present for a future satisfaction or because he has no sense of the future. He is therefore radically improvident: whatever he cannot consume immediately he considers valueless. His bodily needs (especially for sex) and his taste for 'action' take precedence over everything else—and certainly over any work routine. He works only as he must to stay alive, and drifts from one unskilled job to another, taking no interest in the work."[3]

Professor Banfield does not attempt to offer precise estimates of the number of such lower-class individuals, though he does tell us at one point that "such ['multiproblem'] families constitute a small proportion both of all families in the city (perhaps 5 percent at most) and of those with incomes below the poverty line (perhaps 10 to 20 percent). The problems that they present are out of proportion to their numbers, however; in St. Paul, Minnesota, for example, a survey showed that 6 percent of the city's families absorbed 77 percent of its public assistance, 51 percent of its health services, and 56 percent of its mental health and correction casework services."[4]

Obviously if the "lower class culture" in our cities is as persistent and intractable as Professor Banfield contends (and no one can doubt the fidelity of his portrait of a sizable group), it sets a limit on what reasonable antipoverty measures can accomplish.

3. *Ibid.*, p. 53.
4. *Ibid.*, p. 127.

Merit vs. "Luck"

In judging any program of relief, our forefathers usually thought it necessary to distinguish sharply between the "deserving" and the "undeserving" poor. But this, as we have seen, is extremely difficult to do in practice. And it raises troublesome philosophic problems. We commonly think of two main factors as determining any particular individual's state of poverty or wealth—personal merit and "luck." "Luck" we tacitly define as anything that causes a person's economic (or other) status to be better or worse than his personal merits or efforts would have earned for him.

Few of us are objective in measuring this in our own case. If we are relatively successful, most of us tend to attribute our success wholly to our own intellectual gifts or hard work; if we have fallen short in our worldly expectations, we attribute the outcome to some stroke of bad luck, perhaps even chronic bad luck. If our enemies (or even some of our friends) have done better than we have, our temptation is to attribute their superior success mainly to good luck.

But even if we could be strictly objective in both cases, is it always possible to distinguish between the results of "merit" and "luck"? Isn't it luck to have been born of rich parents rather than poor ones? Or to have received good nurture in childhood and a good education rather than to have been brought up in deprivation and ignorance? How wide shall we make the concept of luck? Isn't it merely a man's bad luck if he is born with bodily defects—crippled, blind, deaf, or susceptible to some special disease? Isn't it also merely bad luck, then, if he is born with a poor intellectual inheritance—stupid, feeble-minded, an imbecile? But then, by the same logic, isn't it merely a matter of good luck if a man is born talented, brilliant, or a genius? And if so, is he to be denied any credit or merit for being brilliant?

We commonly praise people for being energetic or hard-working, and blame them for being lazy or shiftless. But may not these qualities themselves, these differences in degrees of energy, be just as much inborn as differences in physical or mental strength or weakness? In that case, are we justified in praising industriousness or censuring laziness?

However difficult such questions may be to answer philosophically, we do give definite answers to them in practice. We do not criticize people for bodily defects (though some of us are not above deriding them), nor do we (except when we are irritated) blame them for being hopelessly stupid. But we do blame them for laziness or shiftlessness, or penalize them for it, because we have found in practice that people do usually respond to blame and punishment, or praise and reward, by putting forth more effort than otherwise. This is really what we have in mind when we try to distinguish between the "deserving" and the "undeserving" poor.

Effect on Incentives

The important question always is the effect of outside aid on incentives. We must remember, on the one hand, that extreme weakness or despair is not conducive to incentive. If we feed a man who has actually been starving, we for the time being probably increase rather than decrease his incentives. But as soon as we give an idle able-bodied man more than enough to maintain reasonable health and strength, and especially if we continue to do this over a prolonged period, we risk undermining his incentive to work and support himself. There are unfortunately many people who prefer near-destitution to taking a steady job. The higher we make any dole or any guaranteed floor under incomes the larger the number of people who will see no reason either to work or to save. The cost to even a wealthy community could ultimately become ruinous.

An "ideal" assistance program, whether private or governmental, would (1) supply everyone in dire need, through no fault of his own, enough to maintain him in reasonable health; (2) would give nothing to anybody not in such need; and (3) would not diminish or undermine anybody's incentive to work or save or improve his skills and earning power, but would hopefully even increase such incentives.

But these three aims are extremeley difficult to reconcile. The nearer we come to achieving any one of them fully, the less likely we are to achieve one of the others. Society has found no perfect solution to this problem in the past, and seems unlikely to find one in the future. The best we can look forward to, I suspect, is some never-quite-satisfactory compromise.

Fortunately, in the United States the problem of relief (not-withstanding the current hysteria of the New Left) is now merely a residual problem, likely to be of constantly diminishing importance as, under free enterprise, we constantly increase total production. The real problem of poverty is not a problem of "distribution" but of production. The poor are poor not because something is being withheld from them, but because, for whatever reason, they are not producing enough. The only permanent way to cure their poverty is to increase their earning power.

CHAPTER 18

The Role of Government

Should the government take positive measures in the effort to eliminate or alleviate poverty? If so, what should these measures be?

This is the most troublesome problem that the student of poverty is called upon to solve.

A large part of our previous discussion has been devoted to explaining what the government should *not* do in the effort to mitigate poverty. It should refrain from adopting measures that impede or discourage the full functioning of the free competitive enterprise system—the system that tends to maximize production, to distribute that production among the tens of thousands of commodities and services in the proportions in which these are socially demanded, to maximize the accumulation of capital and new investment, and so to maximize wages and employment and open up opportunities to all.

Now nine-tenths of the economic regulations that governments have adopted and are still adopting today are at best shortsighted measures that do tend to impede or discourage the functioning of the market. Hence they tend to increase or prolong poverty rather than reduce it. If we could get governments simply to refrain from inflationary, socialist, and destructionist policies we might solve nine-tenths of the problems of poverty that are responsive to political action. Yet the question whether the government should undertake "positive" measures—and if so, which—would remain.

The answer we give to this question must depend in part upon our answer to much broader questions: What is the legitimate province of government? What are the desirable limits to that province?

The most necessary function of government is to protect its citizens against force and fraud; but it does not follow that this is the sole legitimate function. John Stuart Mill in his *Principles of Political Economy* in 1848[1] made an instructive distinction between the *necessary* and the *optional* functions of government. The term "optional" was not meant to imply that it is a matter of indifference or of arbitrary choice whether the government should take these functions upon itself, "but only that the expediency of its exercizing them does not amount to necessity, and is a subject on which diversity of opinion does or may exist."

Among these "optional" functions Mill cited the laws of inheritance, the question of succession in the absence of a will; the definition of property; the obligation imposed on people to perform their contracts; the enforcement of contracts; the determination of what contracts are or are not fit to be enforced (for example, if a man sells himself to another as a slave, or binds himself to lifelong employment in the service of another); the establishment of civil tribunals, of rules of evidence, of prescribed forms of contracts and requirements of witnesses; the registry of births, deaths, marriages, wills, contracts, and

1. Vol. II, Book V, Chs. I and IX.

188

deeds; the provision of guardians for infants and lunatics; coining money; prescribing a set of standard weights and measures; making or improving harbors, building lighthouses, making surveys in order to have accurate maps and charts, raising dykes to keep the sea out, and embankments to keep rivers in; paving, lighting, and cleaning the streets.

Most readers today would accept not only the existence of such "optional" functions of government but the usefulness of the specific examples that Mill cites. Yet few libertarians will follow him when he goes on to declare that these examples "might be indefinitely multiplied without intruding on any disputed ground," and that the only justification needed for any specific government interference is its own individual "expediency."

There are, on the contrary, the strongest general reasons why every proposed extension of governmental interference or power should be scrutinized with jealous vigilance. We know that the more things a government, like an individual, attempts to do, the worse it is likely to do any one of them. We know that all power tends to be abused, and that the greater the power the greater the liability to abuse. We know that power begets power —that the more power a government already has over the lives and activities of its citizens, the more they can be intimidated, and the more easily can it seize still further powers.

Is Relief a Duty of Government?

A book on poverty is of course not the appropriate place to pursue at excessive length the question of the proper sphere of government. But at least some consideration of this broader problem seems a necessary preliminary to an answer to the narrower and relevant question, whether the government should itself provide any assistance or relief to the destitute or starving, or whether it should leave all this to private charity.

The history of the answers to this question is less instructive than one could wish. We find instances of government relief to the needy almost as far back as written history extends. We find systematized state relief in ancient Rome, and in England since the days of Elizabeth. And we find that, for almost as long as this, thoughtful men have been questioning the wisdom of this relief.

In the early nineteenth century economists like Malthus and Ricardo denounced the poor laws of their day on the ground that they tended to bring overpopulation and to undermine production. In 1817 we find Ricardo writing:

"The clear and direct testimony of the poor laws is . . . not, as the legislature benevolently intended, to amend the condition of the poor, but to deteriorate the condition of both poor and rich; instead of making the poor rich, they are calculated to make the rich poor. . . . No scheme for the amendment of the poor laws merits the least attention which has not their abolition for its ultimate object."[2]

When we come to the middle of the nineteenth century, however, we find even the usually uncompromising French economist Bastiat giving guarded approval to emergency government relief:

"If the socialists mean that under extraordinary circumstances, for urgent cases, the state should set aside some resources to assist certain unfortunate people, to help them to adjust to changing conditions, we will, of course, agree. This is done now; we desire that it be done better. There is, however, a point on this road that must not be passed. . . ."[3]

In the early twentieth century we can be confident that F. W. Taussig was speaking for the overwhelming majority of contemporary economists when he wrote: "Some provision for the relief of the indigent there will always have to be."[4] And when

2. David Ricardo, *Principles of Political Economy and Taxation,* 1817. Everyman's Library, pp. 61–62.
3. Frederic Bastiat, *Selected Essays on Political Economy,* Princeton, N.J.: Van Nostrand, 1964, p. 120.
4. F. W. Taussig, *Principles of Economics,* Macmillan, 1921, Vol. II, p. 369.

we get to 1960 we find even a strong libertarian like Professor Hayek writing: "In the Western world some provision for those threatened by the extremes of indigence or starvation due to circumstances beyond their control has long been accepted as a duty of the community. . . . The necessity of some such arrangement in an industrial society is unquestioned—be it only in the interest of those who require protection against acts of desperation on the part of the needy."[5]

A Mid-nineteenth Century Answer

The report of the royal commission on the amendment of the poor laws in 1832, and the subsequent law of 1834, mark a turning point in English thought on the subject; and John Stuart Mill's discussion in the mid-nineteenth century probably summarizes the orthodox view then prevailing among economists. It may make an instructive take-off point for discussion even today.

The difficulty of leaving relief entirely to private charity, as Mill pointed out, is that such charity operates "uncertainly and casually . . . lavishes its bounty in one place, and leaves people to starve in another."[6]

Mill's argument has great weight. In some emergencies help ought, if possible, to be certain and immediate, not left to chance. Take a case of common and almost daily occurrence in any great city. A child playing in the street is hit by an automobile, seriously injured, and knocked unconscious. Are we, before doing anything, to wait until he has been identified, until his parents have been located, until they have guaranteed payment for his treatment, or until some passing stranger magnanimously offers to assume the burden? Or should we have made provision for such cases in advance, so that a police car

5. F. A. Hayek, *The Constitution of Liberty*, University of Chicago Press, 1960, p. 285.
6. This and other quotations from Mill in this chapter are from *Principles of Political Economy*, 1848, etc. II, Book V, Chapters 8 and 11.

or an ambulance can be immediately summoned, and he can be rushed off to a hospital, public or private, with the question of payment to be settled later, even if it should eventually fall on the taxpayers? Very few persons would hesitate, I think, about which answer to give to these questions.

Most persons would also agree that in the event of some natural disaster, such as a tornado, a flood, or an earthquake, the government should rush emergency help to the victims, with the burden of its cost falling on the whole body of the taxpayers.

But then, what about individual cases that involve not merely temporary emergencies, but long-term or even life-long emergencies? What about the person who has fallen seriously ill, or has suffered an injury that will take long to heal, and is without resources? Or what about the blind, or the totally disabled, or the feeble-minded or insane, or those so old and weak that they are no longer able to support themselves and have run out of resources? Perhaps in most cases near relatives could be held legally responsible for their care. But what of the cases where this could not be done, or where the relatives could not be found? Once more, I think, the overwhelming majority of men and women would agree that these persons should not be allowed to starve or die, that their individual fates should not be left to the accidents of haphazard private charity, but that systematic provision should be made for such cases at the public expense.

But now we come to the more difficult cases. What about the able-bodied destitute? What about those who are physically able to work but are out of jobs because they are incompetent, or because they have just been laid off for some reason beyond their control, or because they have not found a job that utilizes their acquired skills, or with the conditions and prestige and pay that they would like, or because they just don't like work— or for a hundred reasons in between? Help in such cases could be "deserved" or "undeserved"; but the first question to be answered is whether able-bodied persons should be given public relief at all.

Mill offers a powerful argument why they should be: "Since the state must necessarily provide subsistence for the criminal poor while undergoing punishment, not to do the same for the poor who have not offended is to give a premium on crime." Another reason he offers for providing subsistence to the destitute able-bodied by law is that if the poor were left to individual charity a vast amount of mendicity would be inevitable.

But if the destitute are to be provided for by the state, how great should this provision be? Here Mill expressed his agreement with the principles embodied in the Poor Law Amendments of 1834. The help should be enough to provide subsistence, no more, no less:

"The state must act by general rules. It cannot undertake to discriminate between the deserving and the undeserving indigent. It owes no more than subsistence to the first, and can give no less to the last."

The task of distinguishing between the deserving and the undeserving, Mill continues, must be left to private charity, which can make these distinctions because it is bestowing its own money, and is entitled to do so according to its own judgment. But:

"The dispensers of public relief have no business to be inquisitors. . . . [They] ought not to be required to do more for anybody, than that minimum which is due even to the worst. If they are, the indulgence very speedily becomes the rule, and refusal the more or less capricious or tyrannical exception."

There are other reasons why the amount of public charity extended to any individual must be held to a minimum. Any state help is bound to be harmful that leaves an idle able-bodied man as well off as he would be if he were working at the market wage for unskilled labor. Government relief should always leave a man with a strong motive to do without it if he can. This was the explicit principle emphasized by the Royal Commission that proposed the 1834 Poor Law. As Mill put it, "If the condition of a person receiving relief is made as eligible as that of a laborer who supports himself by his own exertions, the system strikes at the root of all individual industry and self-government."

Therefore, consistent with providing a minimum for subsistence, the condition of those who are supported by legal charity should be kept considerably less desirable than the condition of those who support themselves.

In keeping with this principle, the Poor Law of 1834 stipulated that relief for the able-bodied could only be provided in workhouses. The people in these workhouses were to be set to monotonous and unattractive work, whether useful or not. This requirement was believed to provide a test that would separate those really in need from those who were not. It was assumed that any man in actual fear of starvation would accept these conditions, and that if he refused to do so it was because he thought a more acceptable alternative—perhaps even taking a "menial" private job—was open to him.

Public opinion today refuses to consider the return of the workhouse. But what is the practicable alternative? As we have already seen in the chapter on "The Fallacy of 'Providing Jobs,' " the government should not attempt to guarantee useful and profitable work, nor provide it directly, nor compel it. (It may require a relief recipient to "register" for a job, or bribe him to take a "job-training" course, but in practice these have proved to be in the main perfunctory gestures.) The only effective way the government has of putting pressure on a relief recipient to keep seeking work is to keep its relief level significantly below what he could earn from taking even a "menial" job.

The Dilemma of Relief

Government relief is on the horns of a dilemma. On the one hand it must try to provide "adequate" subsistence. On the other hand, this should not be so "adequate" that the recipient is content to accept it as a way of life in preference to working. As Mill stated the problem:

194

"In all cases of helping, there are two sets of consequences to be considered: the consequences of the assistance itself, and the consequences of relying on the assistance. The former are generally beneficial, but the latter, for the most part, injurious. ... The problem to be solved is therefore one of peculiar nicety as well as importance: how to give the greatest amount of needful help, with the smallest encouragement to undue reliance on it."

It is my own reluctant conclusion that this problem will never be satisfactorily solved. The more "adequate" we make relief, the more people we are going to find willing to get on it and stay on it indefinitely. The more we try to make sure that everybody really in need of relief gets it, the more certain we can be that we are also giving it to people who neither need nor deserve it. The more we try to make sure, on the other hand, that no loafers or cheaters get on the relief rolls, the more certain we can be that we are also keeping some of the really needy off the relief rolls. A relief system, at best, is bound to be an uneasy compromise between too many and too few, too much and too little.

If I have cited the Poor Law of 1834 or have been quoting from older writers so much—particularly from Mill—it has been to show that our forebears of more than a century ago recognized the two sides of the problem; and that our modern reformers, who so preen themselves on their superior "compassion" and "social conscience," have discovered nothing new, but have merely chosen to shut their eyes to one side of the problem, with increasingly ominous consequences.

Some Ways to Minimize Abuses

If there is no fully satisfactory solution, the problem remains of finding the least unsatisfactory one—perhaps it would be better to say, the least unsatisfactory *package* of solutions. Let us look at some of the more awkward problems.

Much the fastest growing relief program in the United States today has been Aid to Families with Dependent Children (AFDC), on which a mother and her children, legitimate or illegitimate, become eligible for AFDC relief if there is no employed father present. This program has probably encouraged more cheating than all the others put together. It promotes both a real and a feigned break-up of families. Many fathers only pretend to "desert" so that the mothers can collect the relief check.

Yet the program goes on growing because of the difficulties of detecting and proving fraud, and on the argument that in any case children must not be made to suffer for the sins of the parents. On the same argument women get just as much relief for the support of their illegitimate as of their legitimate children. One consequence is to subsidize, encourage, and reward bastardy and the breeding of more children than pauper parents could otherwise support. In 1971, in New York City, more than 70 percent of births to mothers on welfare were outside of wedlock.[6]

The problem is a difficult one, but at least one or two provisions suggest themselves that would restrict its extent. One would be to limit any welfare payment to no more, and preferably less, than a father could earn if he were employed at low-skilled work. Or for the state to make no additional payment for the support of any child beyond, say, the second or third. Or to reduce the definition of a dependent child from the present age of 18 to 16 or 14. Or some combination of such cut-off points.

If it is replied that such restrictions would inflict great hardship in some cases, the answer is that to retain some incentive to self-help, and to avert national bankruptcy, some limit, somewhere, must be put on eligibility to relief and on the amount paid to any single family.

Any relief payment above the minimum necessary for sub-

6. Study reported by *New York Times*, March 21, 1972.

sistence, or any relief to meet specially "deserving" cases, should be left to private charity. In fact, some private charitable organizations could well make it their special function to encourage public agencies to refer to them relief cases that might require supplementary aid, to allow the private group to deal with each such case on its merits. And the reformers who are most distressed by these cases would then have an opportunity to contribute their own voluntary funds for this supplementary help.

Another major welfare problem: Should the burden of relief fall solely on the cities and localities, or should the states or even the Federal government assume part or even the whole of it?

This question has increasingly been answered in the last three or four decades in favor of transferring more and more of the burden to the Federal Government. The result has been that eligibility for relief has been constantly widened and the level of relief constantly raised. Obviously every time eligibility is broadened and every time welfare payments are increased, more people become relief clients.

Far from relieving the states and localities from part of the relief burden, "revenue-sharing" tends to increase it enormously. We have already seen in Chapter 9 that though the Federal contribution to direct relief increased from only 5 percent in 1936 to 53 percent in 1971, the burden on the states and cities went up from $330 million in 1936 to $8,700 million in 1971—a 26-fold increase.

All this could have been foreseen by elementary economic deduction or a little knowledge of the history of the problem. As Ricardo wrote in 1817:

"It would not only be no improvement, but it would be an aggravation of the distress which we wish to see removed, if the fund [from which the poor are supported] were increased in amount or were levied according to some late proposals, as a general fund from the country at large. The present mode of its

197

collection and application has served to mitigate its pernicious effects. Each parish raises a separate fund for the support of its own poor. Hence it becomes an object of more interest and more practicability to keep the rates low than if one general fund were raised for the relief of the poor of the whole kingdom. A parish is much more interested in an economical collection of the rate, and a sparing distribution of relief, when the whole saving will be for its own benefit, than if hundreds of other parishes were to partake of it. It is to this cause that we must ascribe the fact of the poor laws not having yet absorbed all the net revenue of the country; it is to the rigor with which they are applied that we are indebted for their not having become overwhelmingly oppressive. If by law every human being wanting support could be sure to obtain it, and obtain it in such a degree as to make life tolerably comfortable, theory would lead us to expect that all other taxes together would be light compared with the single one of poor rates."[7]

One of the arguments against leaving the payment of relief entirely to the cities or the states is that the payments are then not "uniform" throughout the country. But this is precisely what they should not be. According to official estimates the median money income of families in Mississippi is only 42 percent of the median in Connecticut—or, to put it the other way, the median family income in Connecticut is nearly two and a half times that of Mississippi. A relief payment level suitable to Connecticut and most other Northern States might be so high in the Southern rural states as to tempt millions off their more poorly paid jobs and permanently onto the relief rolls.

But existing public opinion, existing Federal legislation, and court decisions holding it "unconstitutional" even for cities to impose their previous residential requirements on relief applicants, now make it politically all but impossible to go back to

7. *Op. cit.*, pp. 62–63.

the old system under which cities and counties were responsible for their own relief programs.

To come to another major problem: Should applicants for relief be obliged to prove unemployment or poverty—in other words, submit to a means test? The answer is Yes. The argument that such a test is "demeaning and humiliating" will not hold water. It is no more demeaning and humiliating than the investigation that income-tax payers are routinely and systematically put through to prove they did not lie or cheat in making out their reports. The absence of a means test opens the door to almost unlimited fraud. Reformers often tell us that people should be allowed to apply for and stay on relief "without loss of dignity or self-respect." Of course they should never be subjected to any *unnecessary* loss of dignity. But if there is to be no loss *whatever* of dignity or self-respect in getting and staying on relief, then there can be no gain in dignity or self-respect in making some sacrifices to keep off.

Still another problem of relief is whether it should be given in cash or kind. Most present opinion seems to favor giving practically all of it in cash. The argument is that the poor know their own relative needs better than anybody else, and know how to apportion their own expenditures accordingly. The further argument is often added that to restrict the poor mainly to relief in kind is to put an unwarranted restraint on their liberty.

Both of these arguments are fallacious. The sad truth is that one of the reasons people have to go on relief in the first place is that they have been as incompetent or heedless in spending money as in earning it. The worst thing one can give a spendthrift, a drunkard, a drug addict, or a compulsive gambler is cash. The taxpayer has at least the right to an assurance that his money will be used to rehabilitate the pauper and to help his wife and children. Administrative practicalities have to be considered, of course, but so far as possible relief should be paid not in cash, but in the form of non-transferable food stamps, clothing coupons, and the like, with the pauper's rent paid di-

rectly to his landlord, leaving him a minimum for liquor, ciga-
rettes, sex, or TV and stereo sets.

Until quite recently, "liberals" would have considered such a
proposal shocking; but in 1972 even the Human Resources Ad-
ministrator of New York City, Jule M. Sugarman (never previously accused of lack of sympathy for relief applicants), pro-
tested that the disruption and expense generated by the rapidly
expanding number of drug addicts on welfare threatened to
"paralyze" the city's welfare system. Many of these addicts, in
addition to harrassing and committing acts of violence against
both welfare administrators and other welfare recipients, were
using their relief checks to support their drug habits. As one
way to cut back on fraud and drug purchases, Mr. Sugarman
said his agency was considering paying addicts in nonnegotia-
ble scrip and food stamps.[8]

The argument that the relief recipient has some sort of
"right" to get his relief entirely in the form of cash, and should
have complete "freedom to spend," is wholly misdirected. It is
the liberty of the taxpayers who are having part of their earnings seized to support the reliefers that deserves some consideration.

Case of the Permanent Pauper

Still another problem: What is to be done about the able-
bodied pauper and his or her family who tend to stay on relief
indefinitely?

(It seems to me not only desirable but necessary, in the interest of clarity and precision, to revive the word *pauper* in its
specific eighteenth- and nineteenth-century sense, which was,
according to the Oxford English Dictionary, not merely a poor
person, but [since 1775] "a person in receipt of poor-law relief."
Our politicians and many of our newspapers today, searching
for euphemisms, habitually refer to persons on relief simply as

8. *New York Times,* March 16, 1972.

"the poor." This is not only misleading, but unjust to the self-supporting poor, many of whom are even less well off than many on relief.)

We noted in the chapter on "Welfarism Gone Wild" that AFDC families are on relief for an *average* of twenty-three months, that a third of them have been on for three years or more, and that some families have been on relief for three generations. When we are dealing with the blind or the disabled, indefinitely prolonged help may seem unavoidable; but when we are dealing with the able-bodied, such prolonged dependence is a violation of the sound rule that public support should at most be temporary and confined to emergencies.

Suppose we have an able-bodied pauper (with a wife and children, to make the problem harder) who has been on relief for more than a year, who has refused to look seriously for work, who has turned down jobs offered to him on the ground that the pay was too low, or that the jobs were "menial" or vaguely "unsuitable." Can we simply drop him from relief, and take the chance that he and his family will "starve"? No one likes to answer a blunt Yes to this question, and it is long since any politican has dared to do so. But unless a welfare program is allowed to grow utterly beyond control, this is the answer that *at some point* we are compelled to give. Where is that point to be?

First, it ought to go without saying that there should be a constant re-examination by the relief administrators of the condition of relief recipients and their eligibility for continued assistance. This might be only once a year for, say, the blind or totally disabled, but much more often for the able-bodied on general assistance. If an able-bodied man has been on relief, say, for six months, and has repeatedly shown no inclination to look for or accept work, he should be dropped from the rolls and referred to some private charity. The private charity organization, and the man himself, would then have an opportunity to examine his case afresh and see what could be done to make him self-supporting. If, after a few weeks, the private group could find no other solution, they might or might not recommend that he be reinstated on public relief. Some similar process might be applied to Aid to Families with Dependent Children. At the very least, even such a temporary removal from the relief rolls might help to shake the pauper and his family out of a complacent and chronic acceptance of public support in idleness.

Many students of the problem would no doubt like to see even more drastic measures to terminate indefinite relief to the able-bodied. I suspect myself that even if all the proposals I have been making here were adopted—for a means test and other protections against fraud; for payments in kind, where possible, instead of in cash; for stricter limitations on the size of the relief payment to any individual and of the period over which such a payment is made—the reforms even collectively might still prove inadequate to halt the now ever-growing burden of relief.

Perhaps it is even a mistake for a book on the general problem of poverty to discuss the details of relief administration. Those who ought to be best qualified to suggest such reforms are the relief administrators themselves, who are daily immersed in the problems. But their chronic preoccupation seems to be wholly with the immediate interests of their "clients," with hardly a thought to the long-term interests of the economy, of the taxpayers, or of the paupers themselves. The serious student of the problem of poverty must keep in mind that relief is never a solution, but at best a makeshift, and he must continuously devote part of his attention to the most promising ways of minimizing its amount and duration.

Should Relief Recipients Vote?

There is one political change that is practically imperative if a nation is not to be driven toward bankruptcy by relief and redistribution programs completely out of control. This is to suspend the right-to-vote of anybody on public relief.

The argument for this reform was succinctly stated by John Stuart Mill in his *Representative Government* in 1861:

"I regard it as required by first principles that the receipt of parish relief should be a preemptory disqualification for the franchise. He who cannot by his labor suffice for his own support has no claim to the privilege of helping himself to the money of others. By becoming dependent on the remaining members of the community for actual subsistence, he abdicates his claim to equal rights with them in other respects."

Mill even went further, and argued that no one should have the right to vote unless he paid direct taxes:

"It is also important that the assembly which votes the taxes, either general or local, should be elected exclusively by those who pay something towards the taxes imposed. Those who pay no taxes, disposing by their votes of other people's money, have every motive to be lavish and none to economize. . . . It amounts to allowing them to put their hands into other people's pockets for any purpose which they think fit to call a public one."

A century more of popular government has completely verified Mill's fears.

His argument could be extended. There is a crucial difference between an unrestricted "right to vote" and the right, say, peaceably to conduct one's own life without outside interference. For one man's vote may affect not only his own future but that of others. Through it he exercises power over the whole community, a power that ought not to be granted to those who have shown incapacity to provide for even their own elementary needs. Few people today consider it an intolerable abridgment of freedom to restrict the issuance of driving licenses to those who have demonstrated both the skill to drive a car and the responsible use of it. The community is warranted, on the same grounds, in restricting the right to vote to those who have shown sufficient intelligence and responsibility not to steer the ship of state on to the rocks. Nearly every country does, in fact, insist that every voter should meet certain qualifications regarding age, literacy, law-abidance, and sanity. Demonstrated ability to support oneself by one's own efforts would simply add one more essential qualification to the list.

I have one modification to suggest in Mill's proposal. This is that all public aid, whether given in cash or kind, be extended nominally in the form of loans. The recipient would be under no legal obligation to repay such a loan, but until it was repaid he would not be entitled to vote. As an added pressure for reasonably prompt repayment, the loan would bear interest at a rate as high as the government itself was obliged to pay.

This plan would have several advantages. It would help to preserve the self-respect of the applicant for relief. A person who repaid the loan would be able to vote again with his self-esteem intact. He would feel that he had carried his own weight, and had not been a net burden on the community.

For the government too the plan would have several advantages. It would make people more reluctant to go on relief if they could get along without it. It would also make them eager to get off relief as soon as possible so that their debt would not become excessive. For the same reason many would even be willing (which they are not now) to take jobs that paid them very little more than their relief allowance. In brief, they would have more incentive to work. If they were getting, for example, a relief allowance of $60 a week, and were offered a job at $70, they would be less likely to ask themselves (as they do now), "Why should I work for only $10 a week?"

Of course there would always be some people who, perhaps through little fault of their own, had been on the relief rolls so long that repaying their accumulated "loan" and its interest would look like a hopeless task. Any incentive for them to repay in order to be eligible to vote again would be close to nonexistent. It would be advisable, therefore, to provide that anybody who had stayed off relief completely for, say, four or five years, would be eligible to vote again, whether he had repaid his relief loan or not. This would still leave a repayment incentive to anyone whose incurred obligation was so small that he could without great hardship pay it off in less than a year or two.

I am fully aware that, in the present state of public opinion, either Mill's proposal or my suggested amendment of it will be dismissed as "politically impossible." But unless limitations and safeguards similar to those I have been suggesting are soon adopted, the welfare burden will rise to a level that will prove catastrophic.

An Expensive Failure

In the last generation the tendency in the United States and elsewhere has been to try (as President F. D. Roosevelt put it in his message of 1935) to "quit this business of relief" by substituting various forms of "social insurance."

This whole effort has proved a fantastically expensive failure. The so-called "insurance" programs have not only grown at an exponential rate, but degenerated into disguised relief programs—and into relief programs which, in fact, distribute billions of dollars to millions of people in no need of relief. The total national welfare burden has grown more than twenty-nine times since 1935 (from less than $7 billion a year to more than $170 billion in 1971). Yet instead of any of these programs' taking the place of straight relief, that program itself has grown twenty-six times (from $350 million in 1936 to $18,632 million in 1971).

If it were "politically possible," it would be better if all the social welfare programs instituted in the United States since 1935 could be dismantled, and only a reformed relief system remained. We have spent 38 years going in the wrong direction, and getting deeper and deeper into the welfare state quagmire.

The Duty of Providing Education

There is, however, one welfare obligation, older than any except straight relief, that I believe no modern state can escape.

It is in fact assumed today by all but a handful of the poorest and most backward nations. This is the effort to provide an education for every child up to at least some minimum level of literacy.

This is in the interest of every citizen of the state. It helps to increase the productivity and wealth of the whole nation. It makes it easier to teach everyone a skill. When people can at least read signs and elementary directions, it greatly facilitates enforcement of the law. It also makes law abidance more general, when fewer people, because of lack of skill or opportunity, are left in hopeless or desperate circumstances. An educated child is far less likely to be a future relief burden as an adult. Universal education increases equality of opportunity. The education and good nurture of children, far from doing anything to reduce their incentives, tends to increase them. The education of the children of the poor is a true national investment.

There will always be unsettled problems of detail—of the content and length of time of public education. At present, in most of the states, parents are compelled to send children to school from the ages of six or seven to sixteen or seventeen or until they have finished the work of a specified grade, whichever comes first. This education is of course paid for out of general taxation. All states provide elementary and high schools for minors, which they may generally attend at no cost until they graduate or reach the age of twenty-one.

The present tendency has been to carry this even further. Practically all states maintain one or more state universities, sometimes with free tuition. Today the Federal Government grants public money even to most private colleges. The tendency everywhere is to carry public education too far. It is hard to see the justification of providing taxpayers' funds for a higher education that only a small percentage of the population can take advantage of, either intellectually or economically. (In 1968, there were only 30 college students for every 100 persons 18 to 24 years of age.)

The case is strong, in fact, for not carrying state-provided education beyond the grammar-school level, and even stronger for not carrying it beyond the high-school level. As Humboldt pointed out, as long ago as 1792,[9] government-provided education tends at best to hinder variety of individual development, and to impose a deadening uniformity. What he could not foresee, but what is becoming increasingly evident, is that it also tends to encourage or impose the spread of a statist and socialist ideology. Should it be surprising that teachers whose livelihood is dependent on public funds should be prejudiced in favor of the increase in state subsidies and state powers rather than their careful restriction?

Government education, in fact, gets us into the same dilemma as government relief. Once we concede that it ought to be provided at *any* level, where in principle can we draw the lines between what is indispensable, what is enough, and what is too much? And even if we could draw sharp borders theoretically, how, in practice, in democratic countries, can we prevent politicians from appropriating grossly excessive funds for grossly unwarranted purposes?

The Paradox of Relief

The compromise proposals I have been putting forward regarding relief and education are likely to satisfy few. To some they will seem niggardly and lacking in compassion. Others will contend that it is not the proper function of the state to do anything in either field, which should be left wholly to the market or to private charity. I confess I am not too satisfied with my proposals myself. I wish I knew of some indisputable principle which would enable us to draw an exact boundary between what the state should and should not do in these fields, a boundary that would leave no need or room for the exercise of discretion or practical

9. Wilhelm von Humboldt, *The Limits of State Action,* Cambridge University Press, 1969.

judgment. But I have not been able to find any such precise boundary.

Perhaps the problem is that we face here, in fact, a conflict of principles. I have accepted the conclusion (held today by the overwhelming majority not only of the public but of professional economists) that the matter should not be left solely to the uncertainties of haphazard private charity, but that the community has a duty to make some systematic provision for those threatened by the extremes of indigence or starvation owing to circumstances beyond their control. But when we accept the principle that "the State cannot allow anyone to starve," are we not accepting along with it the dubious principle that the State has the right to seize from Peter to compel him to support Paul? And once we concede as a principle that the State may seize money from some to give it to others, what ground of principle have we left to prevent the process from being carried to the point of confiscating all wealth and income above the average in the attempt to bring about full equality—which would only mean, in the end, equality of destitution?

These are troublesome questions, but it may be objected that they are troublesome because of the way they are framed. Does not practically everybody concede that the State does have a right to seize from Peter to pay Paul, when it levies necessary taxes, say, on Peter, a businessman, to pay Paul, a policeman? Is not the real question whether or not Paul is performing necessary and legitimate services in return for payment? Or, even more broadly, is not the real question the long-run political and social consequences of the whole process?

Today, of course, most people would dismiss all these as academic problems. The need of government relief of poverty is generally accepted, and the practical question around which discussion revolves is what form this relief should take and how far it should go.

Regarding the answer to this no two economists seem to agree. My own answer is that government relief, to keep it from getting out of bounds, should be reserved only for catastrophic situations. All relief (except that to the blind, totally disabled, feeble-minded, or very aged) should be only of a temporary and emergency nature.

This relief should never be so low, on the one hand, as to undermine the recipient's health, nor so high, on the other, as to undermine his incentives to self-help and self-support. But these aims will never be completely reconcilable. To the extent that we achieve the one we are unlikely to achieve the other.

Moreover, even a compromise program that may reasonably suit the conditions in one country may prove wholly inapplicable in another. Reformers talk constantly about what governments *should* do about poverty without first asking themselves what a specific government *can* do about poverty. Any relief program must be adjusted to the relative wealth of the country for which it is proposed. It would be quite impossible for India, for example, to adopt a public relief program feasible in the United States. An attempt to ensure everybody in India an income as high as the official U.S. "poverty line" minimum would probably put at least nine-tenths of the Indian population on relief; but there would be no class capable of paying such relief.

This brings us to what I shall call "The Paradox of Relief": *The richer the community, the less the need for relief, but the more it is able to provide; the poorer the community, the greater the need for relief, but the less it is able to provide.*

A less paradoxical way of stating this is that an "adequate" relief system is possible only in a country that is already affluent.

But this takes us back once more to the conclusion that the real solution to the problem of poverty does not lie in any government relief system, in any "welfare program," in any scheme to redistribute wealth or income. It lies in increased production.

One is ashamed to keep repeating anything so obvious, but the only real cure for poverty is the production of wealth.

CHAPTER 19

Private Property, Public Purpose

THE SOCIALISTS AND COMMUNISTS PROPOSE TO CURE POVERTY BY SEIZ-
ing private property, particularly property in the means of production, and turning it over to be operated by the government.

What the advocates of all expropriation schemes fail to realize is that property in private hands used for the production of
goods and services for the market is already for all practical
purposes public wealth. It is serving the public just as much as
—in fact, far more effectively than—if it were owned and operated by the government.

Suppose a single rich man were to invest his capital in a
railroad owned by himself alone. He could not use this merely
to transport his own family and their personal goods. That
would be ruinously wasteful. If he wished to make a profit on
his investment, he would have to use his railroad to transport
the public and their goods. He would have to devote his railroad
to a public use.

And unlike a government agency, the private owner is

obliged by self-preservation to try to avoid losses, which means that he is forced to run his railroad economically and efficiently. And also unlike a government agency, the private capitalist is nearly always obliged to face competition—which means to make the services he provides or the goods he sells superior or at least equal to those provided by his competitors. Therefore the private capitalist normally serves the public far better than the government could if it took over his property. Looked at from the standpoint of the service they provide, the private railroads today are worth vastly more to the public than to their owners.

Though socialists chronically fail to understand it, there is nothing original in the theme just stated. It was hinted at in Adam Smith:

"Every individual is continually exerting himself to find out the most advantageous employment for whatever capital he can command. It is his own advantage, indeed, and not that of the society, which he has in view. But the study of his own advantage naturally, or rather necessarily leads him to prefer that employment which is most advantageous to the society."[1]

At another point Adam Smith was even more explicit:

"Every prodigal appears to be a public enemy, and every frugal man a public benefactor. . . . The principle which prompts to save, is the desire of bettering our condition. . . . An augmentation of fortune is the means by which the greater part of men propose and wish to better their condition. . . . And the most likely way of augmenting their fortune, is to save and accumulate some part of what they desire. . . . [The funds they accumulate] are destined for the maintenance of productive labor. . . . The productive powers of the same number of laborers cannot be increased, but in consequence either of some addition and improvement to those machines and instruments which facilitate and abridge labor; or of a more proper division

1. Adam Smith, *Wealth of Nations,* 1776, Bk. IV, Ch. II.

and distribution of employment. In either case an additional capital is almost always required."[2]

In the history of economic thought, however, it is astonishing how much this truth was neglected or forgotten, even by some of Smith's most eminent successors. But the theorem has been revived, and some of its corollaries more explicitly examined, by several writers in the present century.

Productive Use of Henry Ford's Income

One of them was George E. Roberts, director of the U.S. Mint under three Presidents, who was responsible for the Monthly Economic Letter of the National City Bank of New York from 1914 until 1940.

An example often cited by Roberts was Henry Ford and his automobile plant. Roberts pointed out in the July letter of 1918 that the portion of the profits of Henry Ford's automobile business that he had invested in the development and manufacture of a farm tractor was not devoted to Ford's private wants; nor was that portion which he invested in furnaces for making steel; nor that portion invested in workingmen's houses. "If Henry Ford had exceptional talent for the direction of large productive enterprises the public had no reason to regret that he had an income of $50,000,000 a year with which to enlarge his operations. If that income came to him because he had a genius for industrial management, the results to the public were probably larger than they would have been if the $50,-000,000 had been arbitrarily distributed at 50 cents per head to all the [then, 1918] population of the country."

In brief, only that portion of his income which the owner spends upon his own or his dependents' consumption is devoted to him or to them. All the rest is devoted to the public as completely as though the title of ownership was in the State. The individual may toil, study, contrive and save, but all that he saves inures to others.

2. *Ibid.*, Bk. II, Ch. III.

But the Ford Motor Company, from the profits of which the original owner drew so little for his own personal needs, is not a unique example in American business. Perhaps the greater part of private profits are today reinvested in industry to pay for increased production and service for the public.

Let us see what happened, for example, to all the corporate profits in the United States in 1968, fifty years after George Roberts was writing about the Ford Company. These aggregate net profits amounted before taxes to a total of $88.7 billion (or one eighth of the total national income in that year of $712.7 billion).

Out of these profits the corporations had to pay 46 percent, or $40.6 billion, to the government in taxes. The public, of course, got directly whatever benefit these provided. Corporate profits after taxes then amounted to $48.2 billion, or less than 7 percent of the national income.

These profits after taxes, moreover, averaged only 4 cents for every dollar of sales. This meant that for every dollar that the corporations took in from sales, they paid out 96 cents—partly for taxes, but mainly for wages and for supplies from others.

But by no means all of the $48.2 billion earned after taxes went to the stockholders of the corporations in dividends. More than half—$24.9 billion—was retained or reinvested in the business. Only $23.3 billion went to the stockholders in dividends.

There is nothing untypical in these 1968 corporate reinvestment figures. In every one of the six years preceding 1968 the amount of funds retained for reinvestment exceeded the total amount paid out in dividends.

Moreover, even the $25 billion figure understates corporate reinvestment in 1968. For in that year the corporations suffered $46.5 billion depreciation on their old plant and equipment. Nearly all of this was reinvested in repairs to old equipment or to complete replacement. The $24.9 billion represented reinvestment of profits in *additional* or greatly improved equipment.

And even the $23.3 billion that finally went to stockholders was not all retained by them to be spent on their personal consumption. A great deal of it was reinvested in new enterprises. The exact amount is not precisely ascertainable; but the U.S. Department of Commerce estimates that total personal savings in 1968 exceeded $40 billion.

Thus because of both corporate and personal saving, an ever-increasing supply is produced of finished goods and services to be shared by the American masses.

In a modern economy, in brief, those who save and invest can hardly help but serve the public. As Mises has put it: "In the market society the proprietors of capital and land can enjoy their property only by employing it for the satisfaction of other people's wants. They must serve the consumers in order to have any advantage from what is their own. The very fact that they own means of production forces them to submit to the wishes of the public. Ownership is an asset only for those who know how to employ it in the best possible way for the benefit of the consumers. It is a social function."[3]

The Most Effective Charity

It follows from this that the rich can do most good for the poor if they refrain from ostentation and extravagance, and if instead they save and invest their savings in industries producing goods for the masses.

F. A. Harper has gone so far as to write: "Both fact and logic seem to me to support the view that savings invested in privately owned economic tools of production amount to an act of charity. And further, I believe it to be—as a type—the greatest economic charity of all."[4]

Professor Harper supports this view by quoting from, among

3. Ludwig von Mises, *Human Action*, 3rd Rev. Ed., Chicago: Henry Regnery Co., 1966, p. 684.
4. "The Greatest Economic Charity." Essay in symposium *On Freedom and Free Enterprise*, Mary Sennholz, ed., Van Nostrand, 1956, p. 99.

others, Samuel Johnson, who once said: "You are much surer that you are doing good when you *pay* money to those who work, as a recompense of their labor, than when you *give* money merely in charity."[5]

So, saving and sound investment may be the most important benefit that the rich can confer on the poor.

This theme has found expression in this century by a deplorably small number of writers. One of the most persuasive was Hartley Withers, a former editor of the London *Economist,* who published an ingratiating little book in 1914, a few weeks before the outbreak of the First World War, called *Poverty and Waste.*[6] The contention of his book is that when a wealthy man spends money on luxuries he causes the production of luxuries and so diverts capital, energy, and labor from the production of necessaries, and so makes necessaries scarce and dear for the poor. Withers does not ask him "to give his money away, for he would probably do more harm than good thereby, unless he did it very carefully and skilfully; but only to invest part of what he now spends on luxuries so that more capital may be available for the output of necessaries. So that by the simultaneous process of increasing the supply of capital and diminishing the demand for luxuries the wages of the poor may be increased and the supply of their needs may be cheapened; and he himself may feel more comfortable in the enjoyment of his income."[7]

Yet in spite of the authority of the classical economists and the inherent strength of the arguments for saving and investment, the gospel of spending has an even older history. One of the chief tenets of the "new economics" of our time is that saving is not only ridiculous but the chief cause of depressions and unemployment.

Adam Smith's arguments for saving and investment were at

5. James Boswell, *The Life of Samuel Johnson,* Boston: Charles E. Lauriat Co., 1925, Vol. II, p. 636.

6. Hartley Withers, *Poverty and Waste,* London: Smith, Elder, 1914; 2nd Rev. Ed., John Murray, 1931.

7. *Ibid.,* p. 139.

least partly a refutation of some of the mercantilist doctrines thriving in the century before he wrote. Professor Eli Heckscher, in his *Mercantilism* (Vol. II, 1935), quotes a number of examples of what he calls "the deep-rooted belief in the utility of luxury and the evil of thrift. Thrift, in fact, was regarded as the cause of unemployment, and for two reasons: in the first place, because real income was believed to diminish by the amount of money which did not enter into exchange, and secondly, because saving was believed to withdraw money from circulation."[8]

An example of how persistent these fallacies were, long after Adam Smith's refutation, is found in the words that the sailor-turned-novelist, Captain Marryat, put into the mouth of his hero, Mr. Midshipman Easy, in his novel by that name published in 1836:

"The luxury, the pampered state, the idleness—if you please, the wickedness—of the rich, all contribute to the support, the comfort, and the employment of the poor. You may behold extravagance—it is a vice; but that very extravagance circulates money, and the vice of one contributes to the happiness of many. The only vice which is not redeemed by producing commensurate good, is avarice."

Mr. Midshipman Easy is supposed to have learned this wisdom in the navy, but it is almost an exact summary of the doctrine preached in Bernard Mandeville's *Fable of the Bees* in 1714.

Now though this doctrine is false in its attack on thrift, there is an important germ of truth in it. The rich can hardly prevent themselves from helping the poor to some extent, almost regardless of how they spend or save their money. So far from the wealth of the rich being the cause of the poverty of the poor, as the immemorial popular fallacy has it, the poor are made less poor by their economic relations with the rich. Even if the rich

8. Vol. II, p. 208.

spend their money foolishly and wastefully, they give employment to the poor as servants, as suppliers, even as panderers to their vices. But what is too often forgotten is that if the rich saved and invested their money they would not only give employment to just as many people producing capital goods, but that as a result of the reduced costs of production and the increased supply of consumer goods which this investment brought about, the real wages of the workers and the supply of goods and services available to them would greatly increase.

What is also forgotten by the defenders of luxury spending is that, though it improves the condition of the poor who cater to it, it also increases their dissatisfaction, unrest, and resentment. The result is envy of and sullenness toward those who are making them better off.

From Malthus to Bernard Shaw

The first eminent economist who attempted to refute Adam Smith's proposition that "every prodigal appears to be a public enemy, and every frugal man a public benefactor" was Thomas R. Malthus. Malthus's objections were partly well taken and partly fallacious. I have examined them rather fully in another place;[9] and I shall content myself here with quoting a few lines from the answer that a greater economist than Malthus, David Ricardo, made at the time (circa 1814–21): "Mr. Malthus never appears to remember that to save is to spend, as surely as what he exclusively calls spending. . . . I deny that the wants of consumers generally are diminished by parsimony—they are transferred with the power to consume to another set of consumers."[10]

It remained for a few influential modern writers to launch an all-out attack on saving. One of them was Bernard Shaw. In a

9. *The Failure of the "New Economics,"* Van Nostrand, 1959, pp. 40–43 and 355–362.
10. *Notes on Malthus* (Sraffa edition), p. 449 and p. 309.

shamelessly ignorant and silly book,[11] Shaw actually argued that net saving in a community was not even possible—because food does not keep! "The notion that we could all save together is silly. . . . Peter must spend what Paul saves, or Paul's savings will go rotten. Between the two nothing is saved. The nation as a whole must bake its bread and eat it as it goes along. . . . When you see the rich man's wife (or anyone else's wife) shaking her head over the thriftlessness of the poor because they do not all save, pity the poor lady's ignorance, but do not irritate the poor by repeating her nonsense to them."

Shaw's statement is nonsense compounded. He talks as if men and women, in the Britain and America of 1928, existed at the level of the lower animals, and lived by bread alone. It might have occurred to him that in a modern society food production and food consumption form only a small fraction of total production and consumption. In the United States today, food and beverages account for only 13 percent, or about one eighth, of the gross national product. It should further have occurred to Shaw that even though each individual crop is harvested only during a few weeks of the year, the food supply must be at least sufficiently conserved to last a nation the year round.

And even in the most primitive agricultural societies some food has to be saved even beyond a year, if the society is to survive. The tribe that consumes that part of the corn that it should be setting aside as seed for next year's crop is doomed to starvation.

But neither in a modern nor in a primitive society is it primarily food that is saved from year to year. So far as the individual is concerned, what he nominally saves is money. (This used to consist of the precious metals, gold and silver, which kept extremely well, and did not constantly lose their value like today's universal paper currencies.) What the indi-

11. George Bernard Shaw, *The Intelligent Woman's Guide to Socialism and Capitalism*, Brentano, 1928, p. 7.

vidual really saves is the consumption goods and services he refrains from demanding, so releasing labor and other resources for the production of more and better capital goods. The great bulk of primitive as of modern savings went into improving housing, land, and tools.

Shaw's argument falls into a *reductio ad absurdum* when it proves that there can be no net saving at all by the nation as a whole. What would Shaw make of the present U.S. Department of Commerce figures showing that there is in fact net national saving every year? (In the five years 1967–71 gross private domestic investment averaged annually about 14 percent of the U.S. gross national product.) If Shaw had merely looked around him, he would have seen how saving went into enlarging and improving the nation's productive equipment and into an increase in each decade in labor's productivity and in real wages.

Shaw threw himself into economic controversy all his life; but he never condescended to look up the facts and never understood even some kindergarten economic principles.

We have yet to discuss the views of the most influential opponent of saving in our time—John Maynard Keynes.

It is widely believed, especially by his disciples, that Lord Keynes did not condemn saving until, in a sudden vision on his road to Damascus, the truth flashed upon him and he published it in *The General Theory of Employment, Interest, and Money* in 1936. All this is apocryphal. Keynes disparaged saving almost from the beginning of his career. He was warning his countrymen in a broadcast address in January, 1931, that "whenever you save five shillings, you put a man out of work for a day." And long before that, in his *Economic Consequences of the Peace,* published in 1920, he was writing passages like this:

"The railways of the world which [the nineteenth century] built as a monument to posterity, were, not less than the Pyramids of Egypt, the work of labor which was not free to consume in immediate enjoyment the full equivalent of its efforts.

"Thus this remarkable system depended for its growth on a double bluff or deception. On the one hand the laboring classes accepted from ignorance or powerlessness, or were compelled, persuaded, or cajoled by custom, convention, authority and the well-established order of Society into accepting, a situation in which they could call their own very little of the cake that they and Nature and the capitalists were cooperating to produce. And on the other hand the capitalist classes were allowed to call the best part of the cake theirs and were theoretically free to consume it, on the tacit underlying condition that they consumed very little of it in practice. The duty of 'saving' became nine-tenths of virtue and the growth of the cake the object of true religion. There grew round the nonconsumption of the cake all those instincts of puritanism which in other ages has withdrawn itself from the world and has neglected the arts of production as well as those of enjoyment. And so the cake increased; but to what end was not clearly contemplated. Individuals would be exhorted not so much to abstain as to defer, and to cultivate the pleasures of security and anticipation. Saving was for old age or for your children; but this was only in theory—the virtue of the cake was that it was never to be consumed, neither by you nor by your children after you." (Pp. 19–20.)

This passage illustrates the irresponsible flippancy that runs through so much of Keynes's work. It was clearly written tongue-in-cheek. In the very next sentences Keynes made a left-handed retraction: "In writing thus I do not necessarily disparage the practices of that generation. In the unconscious recesses of its being Society knew what it was about," etc.

Yet he let his derision stand to do its harm.

If we accepted Keynes's original passage as sincerely written, we would have to point out in reply: (1) The railways of the world cannot be seriously compared with the pyramids of Egypt, because the railways enormously improved the production, transportation, and availability of goods and services for the masses. (2) There was no bluff and no deception. The workers who built the railroads were perfectly "free" to consume in immediate enjoyment the full equivalent of their efforts. It was the *capitalist* classes that did nearly all the saving, not the workers. (3) Even the capitalist classes did consume *most* of their slice of the cake; they were simply wise enough to refrain from consuming *all* of it in any single year.

How to Bake a Bigger Cake

This point is so fundamental, and both Keynes and his disciples have so confused themselves and others with their mockery and intellectual somersaults, that it is worth making the matter plain by constructing an illustrative table.

Let us assume that in Ruritania, as a result of net annual saving and investment of 10 percent of output, there is over the long run an average increase in real production of 3 percent a year. Then the picture of economic growth we get over a ten-year period runs like this in terms of index numbers:

Year	Total Production	Consumers' Goods Produced	Capital Goods Produced
First	100	90	10
Second	103	92.7	10.3
Third	106.1	95.5	10.6
Fifth	112.5	101.3	11.2
Tenth	130.5	117.5	13.0

(These results do not differ too widely from what has been happening in recent years in the United States.)

What this table illustrates is that total production in Ruritania increases each year *because of the net saving* (and consequent investment), and would not increase without it. The saving is used year after year to increase the quantity and improve the quality of existing machinery or other capital equipment, and so to increase the output of *both* consumption and capital goods.

Each year there is a larger and larger "cake." Each year, it is true, not all of the currently produced cake is consumed. But there is no irrational or cumulative consumer restraint. For each year a larger and larger cake is in fact consumed; until even at the end of five years (in our illustration), the annual consumers' cake alone is equal to the combined producers' and consumers' cakes of the first year. Moreover, the capital equipment—the ability to produce goods—is now 12 percent greater than in the first year. And by the tenth year the ability to produce goods is 30 percent greater than in the first year; the total cake produced is 30 percent greater than in the first year, and the consumer's cake alone is more than 17 percent greater than the combined consumers' and producers' cakes in the first year.

There is a further point to be taken into account. Our table is built on the assumption that there has been a *net* annual saving and investment of 10 percent a year; but in order to achieve this, Ruritania will probably have to have a *gross* annual saving and investment of, say, twice as much, or 20 percent, to cover the repairs, depreciation and deterioration taking place every year in housing, roads, trucks, factories, equipment. This is a consideration for which no room can be found in Keynes's simplistic and mocking cake analogy. The same kind of reasoning which would make it seem silly to save for new capital would also make it seem silly to save enough even to replace old capital.

In a Keynesian world, in which saving was a sin, production would go lower and lower, and the world would get poorer and poorer.

In the illustrative table I have by implication assumed the long-run equality of saving and investment. Keynes himself shifted his concepts and definitions of both saving and investment repeatedly. In his *General Theory* the discussion of their relation is hopelessly confused. At one point (p. 74) he tells us that saving and investment are "necessarily equal" and "merely different aspects of the same thing." At another point

(p. 21) he is telling us that they are "two essentially different activities" without even a "nexus."

Let us, putting all this aside, try to look at the matter both simply and realistically. Let us define saving as an excess of production over consumption; and let us define investment as the employment of this unconsumed excess to create additional means of production. Then though saving and investment are not always *necessarily* equal, over the long run they tend to equality.

New capital is formed by production combined with saving. Before there can be a given amount of investment, there must be a preceding equal amount of saving. Saving is the first half of the action necessary for more investment. "To complete the act of forming capital it is of course necessary to complement the negative factor of saving with the positive factor of devoting the thing saved to a productive purpose.[12] . . . [But] saving is an indispensable condition precedent to the formation of capital.[13]

Keynes constantly deplored saving while praising investment, persistently forgetting that the second was impossible without the first.

Of course it is most desirable economically that whatever is saved should also be invested, and in addition invested prudently and wisely. But in the modern world, investment follows or accompanies saving almost automatically. Few people in the Western world today keep their money under the floor boards. Even the poorer savers put their money out at interest in savings banks; and those banks act as intermediaries to take care of the more direct forms of investment. Even if a man deposits a relatively large sum in an inactive checking account, the bank in which he deposits, trying always to maximize its profits or to minimize losses, seeks to keep itself "fully loaned up"—

12. Eugen von Böhm-Bawerk, *Positive Theory of Capital,* 1891, South Holland, Ill.: Libertarian Press, 1959, p. 104.
13. *Ibid.,* p. 118.

that is, with close to the minimum necessary cash reserves. If there is insufficient demand at the time for commercial loans, the bank will buy Treasury bills or notes. The result in the United States, for example, is that a bank in New York or Chicago would normally lend out five sixths of the "hoarder's" deposit; and a "country bank" would lend out even more of it.

Of course, to repeat, a saver can do the most economic good, both for himself and his community, if he invests most of his savings, and invests them prudently and wisely. But—contrary to the message of the mercantilists and the Keynesians—even if he "hoards" his savings he may often benefit both himself and the community and at least under normal conditions do no harm.

Three Kinds of Saving

To understand more clearly why this is so it may be instructive to begin by distinguishing between three kinds of (or motives for) saving, and three groups of savers—roughly the poor, the middle class, and the wealthy.

Let us call the most necessary kind, which even the poorest must practice, "rent-day saving." Men buy and pay for things over different time periods. They buy and pay for food, for the most part, daily. They pay rent weekly or monthly. They buy major articles of clothing once or twice a year. A man who earns $10 a day cannot afford to spend $10 a day on food and drink. He can spend on them, say, not more than $6 a day, and must put aside $4 a day from which to pay out part at the end of the month for rent, light, and heat, and another part for a winter overcoat at the end of six months, and so on. This is the kind of saving necessary to ensure one's ability to spend throughout the year. "Rent-day saving" can symbolize all the saving necessary to pay for regularly recurrent and unavoidable living expenses. Obviously this kind of saving, sustained only for weeks or a season, and varying in time as among individuals, can in no circumstances be held responsible for business depressions. It is utter irresponsibility on the part of the Bernard Shaws to ridicule it.

The next kind of saving, which applies especially to the middle classes, is what we may call "rainy-day saving." This is saving against such possible though not inevitable contingencies as loss of a job, illness in the family, or the like.

It is this "rainy-day saving" that the Keynesians most deplore, and from which they fear the direst consequences. Yet even in extreme cases it does not, except in very special cyclical circumstances, tend to bring about any depression or economic slowdown.

Let us consider, for example, a society consisting entirely of "hoarders" or "misers." They are hoarders or misers in this sense: that they all assume they are going to live till 70 but will be forced to retire at 60; and they want to have as much to spend in each of their last ten years as in their 40 working years from 20 to 60. This means that each family will save one fifth of its annual income over 40 years in order to have the same amount to spend in each of its final ten years.

We are deliberately assuming the extreme case, so let us assume that the money saved is not invested in a business or in stocks or bonds, is not even put in a savings bank, earns no interest, but is simply "hoarded."

This of course would permit no economic improvement whatever. But if it were the regular permanent way of life in that community, at least *it would not lead to a depression.* The people who refrained from buying a certain amount of consumers' goods and services would not be bidding up their prices; they would simply be leaving them for others to buy. If this saving for old age were the regular and expected way of life, and not some sudden unanticipated mania for saving, the manufacturers of consumer goods would not have produced an oversupply to be left on their hands; the older people in their seventh decade would in fact be spending more than similarly aged people in a "spending" society, and the unspent savings of those who died would revert to the spending stream. Over a long period, year by year, there would be just as much spent as in a "spending" society.

Let us remember that money saved, in an evenly rotating economy, where there is neither monetary inflation nor deflation, does not go out of existence. Savings, even when they are not invested in production goods, are merely *deferred* or *postponed* spending. The money stays somewhere and is always finally spent. In the long run, in a society with a relatively stable ratio between hoarders and spenders, savings are constantly coming back into the spending stream, through old-age spending or through deaths, keeping the stream at an even flow.

What we are trying to understand is merely the effect of saving *per se,* and not of sudden and unanticipated *changes* in spending and saving. Therefore we are *abstracting* from the effects produced by unexpected changes in spending and saving or changes in the supply of money. If even a heavy amount of saving were the regular way of life in a community, the relative production and prices of consumers' and producers' goods would already be adjusted to this. Of course, if a depression sets in from some other cause, and the prices of securities and of goods begin to fall, and people suddenly fear the loss of their jobs, or a further fall in prices, this may lead to a massive and unanticipated *increase* in saving (or more exactly in nonspending) and this may of course intensify a depression already begun from other causes. But depressions cannot be blamed on regular, planned, anticipated saving.

Some readers may contend that I have not yet imagined the most extreme case of saving—a society, say, all the members of which perpetually save more than half as much as they earn, and keep saving, not for old age, or for any reasonable contingency, but simply because of a "religion" of saving. In brief, these would be the cake nonconsumers of Keynes's satire. But even such an imaginary society involves a contradiction of terms. If the members of that society intended always to live at their existing modest or even mean level, why would they keep exerting themselves to produce more than they ever expected to consume? That would be pathologic to the point of insanity. Keynes's allegory of the extent of supposed nineteenth-century thrift was purely an hallucination.

We come finally to the third type of saving—what we may call "capitalist" saving. This is saving that is put aside for investment in industry—either directly, or indirectly in the form of savings bank deposits. It is saving that yields interest or profits. The saver hopes, in his old age or even earlier, to live on the income yielded by his investments rather than by consuming his saved capital.

This type of "capitalist" saving was until recently confined to the very rich. Indeed, even the very rich were not able to take advantage of this type of saving until the modern development of banks and corporations. As late as the beginning of the eighteenth century we hear of London merchants on their retirement taking a chest of gold coin with them to the country with the intention of gradually drawing on that hoard for the rest of their lives.[14] Today the greater part even of the American middle classes, however, enjoy the advantage of capitalist saving.

To sum up. Contrary to age-old prejudices, the wealth of the rich is not the cause of the poverty of the poor, but helps to alleviate that poverty. No matter whether it is their intention or not, almost anything that the rich can legally do tends to help the poor. The spending of the rich gives employment to the poor. But the saving of the rich, and their investment of these savings in the means of production, gives just as much employment, and in addition makes that employment constantly more productive and more highly paid, while it also constantly in-

14. F. A. Hayek, *Profits, Interest and Investment,* London: George Routledge, 1939, pp. 162–163. See also the numerous cases mentioned in G. M. Trevelyan's *English Social History,* David McKay, 1942.

creases and cheapens the production of necessities and amenities for the masses.

The rich should of course be directly charitable in the conventional sense, to people who because of illness, disability or other misfortune cannot take employment or earn enough. Conventional forms of private charity should constantly be extended. But the most effective charity on the part of the rich is to live simply, to avoid extravagance and ostentatious display, and to save and invest so as to provide more people with increasingly productive jobs, and to provide the masses with an ever-greater abundance of the necessities and amenities of life.

CHAPTER 20

The Cure for Poverty

THE THEME OF THIS BOOK IS THE CONQUEST OF POVERTY, NOT ITS "abolition." Poverty can be alleviated or reduced, and in the Western world in the last two centuries it has been almost miraculously alleviated and reduced; but poverty is ultimately individual, and individual poverty can no more be "abolished" than disease or death can be abolished.

Individual or family poverty results when the "breadwinner" cannot in fact win bread; when he cannot or does not produce enough to support his family or even himself. And there will always be some human beings who will temporarily or permanently lack the ability to provide even for their own self-support. Such is the condition of all of us as young children, of many of us when we fall ill, and of most of us in extreme old age. And such is the permanent condition of some who have been struck by misfortune—the blind, the crippled, the feeble-minded. Where there are so many causes there can be no all-embracing cure.

It is fashionable to say today that "society" must solve the problem of poverty. But basically each individual—or at least each family—must solve its own problem of poverty. The overwhelming majority of families must produce more than enough for their own support if there is to be any surplus available for the remaining families that cannot or do not provide enough for their own support. Where the majority of families do not provide enough for their own support—where society as a whole does not provide enough for its own support—no "adequate relief system" is even temporarily possible. Hence "society" cannot solve the problem of poverty until the overwhelming majority of families have already solved (and in fact slightly more than solved) the problem of their own poverty.

All this is merely stating in another form the Paradox of Relief referred to in Chapter 18: The richer the community, the less the need for relief, but the more it is able to provide; the poorer the community, the greater the need for relief, but the less it is able to provide.

And this in turn is merely another way of pointing out that relief, or redistribution of income, voluntary or coerced, is never the true solution of poverty, but at best a makeshift, which may mask the disease and mitigate the pain, but provides no basic cure.

Moreover, government relief tends to prolong and intensify the very disease it seeks to cure. Such relief tends constantly to get out of hand. And even when it is kept within reasonable bounds it tends to reduce the incentives to work and to save both of those who receive it and of those who are forced to pay it. It may be said, in fact, that practically every measure that governments take with the ostensible object of "helping the poor" has the long-run effect of doing the opposite. Economists have again and again been forced to point out that nearly every popular remedy for poverty merely aggravates the problem. I have analyzed in these pages such false remedies as the guaranteed income, the negative income tax, minimum-wage laws,

laws to increase the power of the labor unions, opposition to labor-saving machinery, promotion of "spread-the-work" schemes, special subsidies, increased government spending, increased taxation, steeply graduated income taxes, punitive taxes on capital gains, inheritances, and corporations, and outright socialism.

But the possible number of false remedies for poverty is infinite. Two central fallacies are common to practically all of them. One is that of looking only at the immediate effect of any proposed reform on a selected group of intended beneficiaries and of overlooking the longer and secondary effect of the reform not only on the intended beneficiaries but on everybody. The other fallacy, akin to this, is to assume that production consists of a fixed amount of goods and services, produced by a fixed amount and quality of capital providing a fixed number of "jobs." This fixed production, it is assumed, goes on more or less automatically, influenced negligibly if at all by the incentives or lack of incentives of specific producers, workers, or consumers. "The problem of production has been solved," we keep hearing, and all that is needed is a fairer "distribution."

What is disheartening about all this is that the popular ideology on all these matters shows no advance—and if anything even a retrogression—compared with what it was more than a hundred years ago. In the middle of the nineteenth century the English economist Nassau Senior was writing in his journal:

"It requires a long train of reasoning to show that the capital on which the miracles of civilization depend is the slow and painful creation of the economy and enterprise of the few, and of the industry of the many, and is destroyed, or driven away, or prevented from arising, by any causes which diminish or render insecure the profits of the capitalist, or deaden the activity of the laborer; and that the State, by relieving idleness, improvidence, or misconduct from the punishment, and depriving abstinence and foresight of the reward, which have

231

been provided for them by nature, may indeed destroy wealth, but most certainly will aggravate poverty."[1]

Man throughout history has been searching for the cure for poverty, and all that time the cure has been before his eyes. Fortunately, as far at least as it applied to their actions as individuals, the majority of men instinctively recognized it—which was why they survived. That individual cure was Work and Saving. In terms of social organization, there evolved spontaneously from this, as a result of no one's conscious planning, a system of division of labor, freedom of exchange, and economic cooperation, the outlines of which hardly became apparent to our forebears until two centuries ago. That system is now known either as Free Enterprise or as Capitalism, according as men wish to honor or disparage it.

It is this system that has lifted mankind out of mass poverty. It is this system that in the last century, in the last generation, even in the last decade, has acceleratively been changing the face of the world, and has provided the masses of mankind with amenities that even kings did not possess or imagine a few generations ago.

Because of individual misfortune and individual weaknesses, there will always be some individual poverty and even "pockets" of poverty. But in the more prosperous Western countries today, capitalism has already reduced these to a merely residual problem, which will become increasingly easy to manage, and of constantly diminishing importance, if society continues to abide in the main by capitalist principles. Capitalism in the advanced countries has already, it bears repeating, conquered *mass* poverty, as that was known throughout human history and almost everywhere, until a change began to be noticeable sometime about the middle of the eighteenth century. Capitalism will continue to eliminate mass poverty in more and more places and to an increasingly marked extent if it is merely permitted to do so.

1. Nassau Senior, *Journal Kept in France and Italy from 1848–52*, London: Henry S. King, 2nd ed. 1871, Vol. I, pp. 4–5.

In the chapter "Why Socialism Doesn't Work," I explained by contrast how capitalism performs its miracles. It turns out the tens of thousands of diverse commodities and services in the proportions in which they are socially most wanted, and it solves this incredibly complex problem through the institutions of private property, the free market, and the existence of money—through the interrelations of supply and demand, costs and prices, profits and losses. And, of course, through the force of competition. Competition will tend constantly to bring about the most economical and efficient method of production possible with existing technology—and then it will start devising a still more efficient technology. It will reduce the cost of existing production, it will improve products, it will invent or discover wholly new products, as individual producers try to think what product consumers *would* buy if it existed.

Those who are least successful in this competition will lose their original capital and be forced out of the field; those who are most successful will acquire through profits more capital to increase their production still further. So capitalist production tends constantly to be drawn into the hands of those who have shown that they can best meet the wants of the consumers.

Perhaps the most frequent complaint about capitalism is that it distributes its rewards "unequally." But this really describes one of the system's chief virtues. Though mere luck always plays a role with each of us, the increasing tendency under capitalism is that penalties are imposed roughly in proportion to error and neglect and rewards granted roughly in proportion to effort, ability, and foresight. It is precisely this system of graduated rewards and penalties, in which each tends to receive in proportion to the market value he helps to produce, that incites each of us constantly to put forth his greatest effort to maximize the value of his own production and thus (whether intentionally or not) help to maximize that of the whole community. If capitalism worked as the socialists think an economic system ought to work, and provided a constant equality of living conditions for all, regardless of whether a man was able or not, resourceful or not, diligent or not, thrifty or not, if capitalism put no premium on resourcefulness and effort and no penalty on idleness or vice, it would produce only an equality of destitution.

Another incidental effect of the inequality of incomes inseparable from a market economy has been to increase the funds devoted to saving and investment much beyond what they would have been if the same total social income had been spread evenly. The enormous and accelerative economic progress in the last century and a half was made possible by the investment of the rich—first in the railroads, and then in scores of heavy industries requiring large amounts of capital. The inequality of incomes, however much some of us may deplore it on other grounds, has led to a much faster increase in the total output and wealth of all than would otherwise have taken place.

Those who truly want to help the poor will not spend their days in organizing protest marches or relief riots, or even in repeated protestations of sympathy. Nor will their charity consist merely in giving money to the poor to be spent for immediate consumption needs. Rather will they themselves live modestly in relation to their income, save, and constantly invest their savings in sound existing or new enterprises, so creating abundance for all, and incidentally creating not only more jobs but better-paying ones.

The irony is that the very miracles brought about in our age by the capitalist system have given rise to expectations that keep running ahead even of the accelerating progress, and so have led to an incredibly shortsighted impatience that threatens to destroy the very system that has made the expectations possible.

If that destruction is to be prevented, education in the true causes of economic improvement must be intensified beyond anything yet attempted.

Index

Johnson, Lyndon B., 32, 72, 83
Johnson, Samuel, 125, 215

Kershner, Howard E., 113n.
Keynes, John Maynard, Lord, 219–227
Keynesianism, 140, 222, 224–225
King, Gregory, 73
Knight, Frank H., 121

Labor unions. *See* Unions
Labor Party, British, 127
Labor-saving machinery, 145, 231
Labor Statistics, Bureau of, 36
Labor theory of value, 156
Laissez-faire, 169, 179
Land reform, 120, 143
Laski, Harold J., 125n.
Latin America, 28, 167
Lawyers, 99
Lend-Lease, 167–168
Levellers, 125
Lloyd George, David, 83, 86
"Lower-class culture," 182–183
Luck, 184–185
Luxuries, 53

Macaulay, Thomas Babington, 159–160
McGovern, Senator George, 120
Malthus, Thomas R., 16, 20–30, 40, 217
Man vs. the Welfare State, 116, 147, 176n.
Mandeville, Bernard, 216
Marginal utilities, 53
Marshall, Alfred, 41, 42n.
Market, free, 124, 152
"Market is color-blind, The," 63
Marryat, Captain Frederick, 216
Marshall, General George C., 168
Marshall Plan, 167–169, 174
Marxist labor theory of value, 156
Meadows, Dennis, 27
Means test, 199
Medicaid, 97, 120
Medicare, 87, 120
Mercantilism, 216
Merit vs. "Luck," 184–185
Michigan, 100
Middle Ages, 14, 15
Middle East, 167
Midshipman Easy, Mr., 216
Mill, John Stuart, 24–25, 56–57, 139–140, 188–189, 191, 193–195, 203–205
Miller, Herman P., 37n., 38n., 50, 55
Minimum wage laws, 63, 107, 147, 230

Mises, Ludwig von, 158n., 214
Model cities, 97
Money, 152, 155, 216, 218
Myrdal, Gunnar, 145

National City Bank, 122n., 123, 212
National Enquirer, 27n.
National Health Service Act, 86
National Insurance Act of 1911 (British), 83, 86
"Negative Income Tax," 116–120, 230
Negroes, 147, 182; economic gains of, 59–65
Neo-Malthusianism, 23, 27, 29
Netherlands, 122
Nevada, 100
New Deal, 72
New Deal in Old Rome, The, 67
New York City, 79, 93, 101–102, 200
New York magazine, 100n.
New York Times, 99n., 101, 103n., 117n., 124n., 196n., 200n.
Newsweek, 101n.
Nixon, President, 27, 88, 91, 104
Norris-LaGuardia Act, 142
Norway, 122
Nutrition, "adequate," 34–35

OASDI program, 89
Office of Economic Opportunity (OEO), 97, 98, 99
Oil companies, 167
Old Age Assistance (OAA), 97, 120, 148, 209
Old Age Pensions Act of 1908 (British), 83
Opinion Research Corporation, 46

Pakistan, 173
Paradox of relief, 207–209
Pareto, Vilfredo, 53
Pareto's Law, 53–54
Passman, Otto E., 170
Paupers, 200–201
Pensions, 86
Perry, Commodore M. C., 161–162
Peru, 173
Phonographs, 51
Pigou, A.C., 54, 106
Point Four, 169–170, 176n.
Poor, "deserving" and "undeserving," 184–186
Poor Laws: Amendment Act of 1834, 74–80, 111, 191, 193–195; Elizabethan, 105; of England, 29, 72–84;

238

reform of 1834, 74–82, 111, 193–195; of Rome, 66–71
Poor Relief in ancient Rome, 66–71. *See also* Relief
Poorer, why some are, 178–186
Population: *Bomb*, 27; *Essay on*, 16, 20–30, 40; growth of, 17, 29; Malthus on, 20–30; and poverty, 20–30; "zero growth," 29
Positive Theory of Capital, 223
Poverty: article on, 180; capitalism as cure for, 232–234; causes of, 178–186; "conditions associated with," 181–182; cure for, 209, 229–234; defining, 31–39; false remedies for, 143–149; individual, 178–186; "line," 209; mass, 232; paradox of, 179; pockets of, 178–179; and population, 20–30; problem of, 13–19, 186, 209; reasons for, 178–186; as residual problem, 18, 232; "threshold," 36, 37, 38, 209; "war on," 32; *and Waste*, 32, 215
Prentice, E. Parmalee, 13, 19
Price and wage controls, 71, 149
Private charity, 191, 197, 201–202, 207, 234
Private property, 124, 152; public purpose, 210–228
Production of wealth, 176, 186, 209, 231, 233
Profits, 45–48, 152, 213, 231; "excessive," 48
Property, private, 124, 152; public purpose, 210–228
Pyramids of Egypt, 219

Radios, 51
Railways, 219, 234
Reagan, Governor Ronald, 100, 102, 103
Redistribution of income or wealth, 113–124, 143, 230–231
Refrigerators, 51
Relief, 93–104, 120, 148; "adequate," 194; cash or kind, 199; dilemma of, 81–84, 194–195; Federal contribution to, 197–199; government role in, 187–209; ideology, 176; in form of loans, 204–205; as makeshift, 202, 230; means test for, 199; paradox of, 207–209, 230; recipients of, 202; uniform, 198. *See also* Welfare
Rent subsidies, 97, 98, 120, 148, 199–200
Representative Government, 203

Revolution, 128; French, of 1789, 128; of 1848, 126
Ricardo, David, 16, 190, 197–198, 217
Rich, as workers, 55
Rich Man, Poor Man, 37n., 38n.
Right to vote, 202–205
Roberts, George E., 212–213
Rome, ancient, famine in, 14; poor relief in, 66–71, 120, 190
Roosevelt, Franklin D., 32, 72, 87, 205
Rostovtzeff, M., 67, 69n., 70
Roth, Wm. V., Jr., 98
Rothbard, Murray C., 121
Royal Commission, report of 1832, 74–83, 191; report of 1905
Ruritania, 221–222
Russia, 17, 18, 19, 151, 154, 167–168, 173
Rustin, Bayard, 61n.

St. Louis, Mo., 93
St. Paul, Minn., 183
Samuelson, Paul, 50
San Francisco, 93, 100
Saving, 214–228, 232, 234; three kinds of, 224–228
Schumpeter, Joseph A., 22
Schoeck, Helmut, 125–126
Self-help, 209
Senior, Nassau W., 74, 80–83, 231–232
Sennholz, Mary, 214n.
Shaw, George Bernard, 217–219, 225
Sickness benefits, 148
Single tax, 121
Slave labor in Rome, 69
Smith, Adam, 24, 41, 160, 211–212, 215–217
Snyder, Carl, 53–54
Snyder, Richard A., 104n.
Social Security, 87–93, 120, 205
Social Security Administration, 33, 181
Socialism, 127, 207, 231; *an Analysis*, 158n.; why it doesn't work, 150–158, 233
Soviet Russia, 17, 18, 19, 151, 154, 167–168, 173
Speenhamland plan, 73, 75
Spending, gospel of, 215, 217, 231
Spread-the-work schemes, 231
State, role of. *See* Government
Strachey, J. St. Loe, 74
Strikes, 133–138, 142
Subsidies, 231. *See also* Rent Subsidies

239

Sugarman, Jule M., 200
Sweden, 122
Switzerland, 122

Taft-Hartley Act, 142
Taussig, F. W., 190
Taxation, 231. *See also* Corporation Income and Income Tax
Taxpayers, 115, 148, 199
Technological progress, 53
Telephones, 51
Television sets, 51
Thornton, William, 139–140
Tiberius, Emperor, 68
Time, 101n.
Time Will Run Back, 158n.
Times, New York. See *New York Times*
Tobin, James, 147
Tocqueville, Alexis de, 128–130
Toilets, 50
Trevelyan, G. M., 73, 227n.
Truman, President Harry S., 169
Turgot, Baron de, 24
"Two Nations," 31

Unemployment "insurance," 86, 90–93, 120, 148
Unheavenly City, The, 182n.
Unions, 231; how they reduce wages, 131–142
United Arab Republic, 173
United Kingdom, 122. *See also* England, Great Britain
United Nations, 28
United States, 122, 141, 151, 161, 162, 173, 209, and *passim*
U. S. News & World Report, 101n., 103n.
Upward Bound, 98

Value, labor theory of, 156
Veterans' programs, 97, 120, 148
Victorian Age, 111
VISTA, 97
Vote, and relief recipients, 202–205

Wage-Hour Law, 145–146
Wages, 44, 45; how unions reduce, 131–142; indeterminacy theory, 132
Wagner-Taft-Hartley Act, 142
Walford, Cornelius, 15n.
Wall Street Journal, The, 104n.
War on Poverty, 72, 83
Warner, Professor A. G., 180–181
Washing machines, 51
Wealth: dividing, 113–124, 143; inherited, 55
Webb, Beatrice, 83
Welfare, 94–104. *See also* Relief
Welfare programs, number of, 97–99
Welfare State, 83; ballooning, 85–92
Welfare Myths vs. Facts, 103–104
Welfarism gone wild, 93–104
West Germany. *See* Germany
What You Should Know About Inflation, 149
Will Dollars Save the World?, 174, 176n.
Wirtz, W. Willard, 101
Withers, Hartley, 32n., 215
Wood, John B., 176n.
Wohlfartsstaat, 85
Work, 232
Works Progress Administration (WPA), 109

Youth, rebellious, 19
Yugoslavia, 168